David M. Pyle

# VOLCANOES

## Encounters through the Ages

Bodleian Library
UNIVERSITY OF OXFORD

**For Tamsin, Alice and Dominic; and**
**for everyone on Kamran's Ward**

First published in 2017 by the Bodleian Library
Broad Street, Oxford OX1 3BG

www.bodleianshop.co.uk

ISBN: 978 1 85124 459 1

Text © David M. Pyle, 2017
Images, unless specified, © Bodleian Library,
University of Oxford, 2017

Designed and typeset by Dot Little at the
Bodleian Library in 10.5/15 pt Warnock
Printed and bound by Great Wall Printing Co.
Ltd., Hong Kong on 157 gsm matt art paper

British Library Catalogue in Publishing Data
A CIP record of this publication is available from
the British Library

# CONTENTS

# FOREWORD

Volcanic eruptions and their aftermath have fascinated us for millennia. Whether as signposts to an underworld, beacons to ancient mariners or as an extraordinary manifestation of the natural world, many people have been drawn to volcanoes and have left records of those encounters. This book explores the history of the study of volcanoes. From fragments of scrolls, carbonized in the great eruption of Vesuvius 2,000 years ago, to the first photographs of a volcanic eruption, it brings together records that document, describe and interpret volcanoes and their activity through time.

Britain has no active volcanoes, but has bred many volcanologists. Ancient volcanoes are responsible for some of Britain's most spectacular uplands and island scenery, from the Inner Hebrides to Snowdonia and the central Lake District. To understand these ancient rocks, natural historians have over the centuries travelled all over the world to see volcanoes for themselves. Many of these accounts have contributed immeasurably to our current understanding of volcanoes.

The materials that we have drawn on from Oxford's archives and research collections are dominated by the reports, letters and sketches of European travellers and natural historians. Some travelled for personal gain, looking to map and acquire new territories, lands and resources; others travelled to seek the edges of the known world, as it appeared to Europeans; and still more simply travelled for pleasure, education and personal enrichment. This book explores some of these themes, as well as showing the visual delights, depicted through the ages, of some of the world's most spectacular volcanoes. The Bodleian Libraries would like to express their great thanks to Professor David M. Pyle of Oxford's Department of Earth Sciences, for researching and writing this book, which accompanies an exhibition at the Bodleian, for which he was the lead curator.

**Richard Ovenden**
Bodley's Librarian

Figure 1    Front plate showing styles of eruptive activity at Vesuvius. From the supplement to the 1779 edition of William Hamilton's *Campi Phlegraei*, Oxford, Bodleian Library, Vet. F5 b.2.

# INTRODUCTION

Volcanoes are vivid and dramatic signs that the planet on which we live has a hot and dynamic interior. The volcanoes that we see in the news, on postcards and in children's tales of dinosaurs and tropical islands offer a tiny glimpse of Earth's hidden depths. To scientists, these same volcanoes offer us some clues to how Earth's giant heat engine works. When, as expected, these volcanoes erupt, we get a brutal reminder of the fragile and tenuous existence that humans have on Planet Earth.

In the past, volcanic eruptions were described in letters, manuscript accounts and early printed books, and illustrated through sketches, woodcuts and engravings (Figure 2). Today, anyone with access to the Internet can watch volcanic eruptions as they happen. Earth-observing satellites, in orbit around our planet and bristling with sensors, beam back images in 'near real time' of volcanoes in eruption. Bright-red pixels reveal the hot spots of lava or gas emerging in a volcanic crater, or extruding from cracks in Earth's surface. Snaky tendrils of volcanic ash and sulphurous gases may be swept by winds in the upper reaches of the atmosphere for thousands of kilometres away from the erupting volcano. But even today, these eruptions that we can see tell us about only a small part of the molten rock cycle. For every gobbet of molten rock thrown out by an erupting volcano, at least six remain deep inside the Earth – helping to build the continents that we stand on or the floor of the ocean. For every volcano that we see erupting at the Earth's surface, there are many more eruptions that pass unnoticed on the sea floor, thousands of metres below us. Here, volcanism is helping continuously to create new ocean floor along the great chain of submarine mountain ridges – ocean floor which is recycled hundreds of millions of years later at the trenches that mark the graveyard of the ocean crust.

Volcano scientists are still grappling to answer some of the simplest questions about how the Earth works. When will the next eruption happen? What will happen when it does so? These are the same sorts of questions that people have been asking for millennia. Our present understanding builds on observations of eruptions made by very many people in the past.

Figure 2 Paroxysmal eruption of Vesuvius seen from Naples, 8 August 1779. Gouache by Pietro Fabris in the supplement to William Hamilton's *Campi Phlegraei*, 1779. Oxford, Bodleian Library, Vet. F5 b.2, Tavola II.

The aim of this book is to explore how their representations, descriptions and ideas about volcanoes have helped us to investigate some of the ways that volcanoes behave, and the consequences of that activity. This is not a textbook – there are many excellent books to satisfy the reader who is in search of technical knowledge – and nor is it anything other than selective, in the material used. To help understand the significance of some of the early accounts of eruptions, however, a short explanation of the current ideas about how volcanoes behave, and what they may tell us about the Earth, is necessary.

Geologists – who study the Earth and its history – are used to thinking about the passage of time in hundreds, thousands and millions of years. By the 1870s geologists such as Archibald Geikie, director of the British Geological Survey, were content that all geological history could fit within 'about 100 millions of years of time'.[1] With the discovery of radioactivity as a technique for dating ancient rocks, this was soon extended to billions of years. Geologists are also comfortable with treating the very physical objects that we stand on – soil, rock, the surface of the planet – as transient materials that tell a story (of how they got to be here), but which will eventually be removed by weathering, erosion or plate tectonics and replaced by something else. Compared with the enormity of the scale of Earth's history – all 4.56 billion years of it – humans have been on the Earth's surface for a very short time; and we only have recorded observations for perhaps the past 2,000 years. Imagine watching a movie of the whole of Earth's history compressed into two hours. The fraction of time taken to show the last two frames is equivalent to the length of time that modern humans have lived on Earth; while the last frame spans the 20,000 years that have passed since the peak of the last ice age.

## Volcanoes and the heat of the Earth

Earth is a giant heat engine. The amounts of heat escaping out of the Earth at the present day are small compared with the heat from sunlight that arrives at the top of Earth's atmosphere. But some of this heat has been stored since the Earth formed billions of years ago, and is still leaking out today as the Earth's molten core continues to freeze and cool, thousands of kilometres beneath our feet. About half of the heat escaping from the Earth today comes from the deep interior, and has made its way towards the surface by being carried along by the creakingly slow flow of Earth's mantle. The other half of the heat comes

Figure 3    Steaming fumaroles and a cauldron of boiling mud, Iceland. From Mackenzie's *Travels in the island of Iceland*, 1812. Oxford, Bodleian Library, 2043 d.11, plate 8

from the energy released by natural radioactive decay processes of atoms of uranium, thorium and potassium in the outer layers of Earth's crust.

One of the consequences of this movement of heat – and of the fact that the Earth's interior is still hot – is that at depths of between 60 and 100 kilometres below the surface, many rocks are nearly hot enough to melt. At these depths it only takes a geologically small change for rock to start to melt. The one thing that confounds this process is tectonic plates. These plates are, as the name suggests, relatively strong and rigid, and form a cool shell about 100 kilometres thick that surrounds the hot, sticky interior of the planet. The plates are quite similar to the thickness of a chicken's eggshell if we compare Earth to the size of an egg. Earth's surface is made up of about seven major plates, and a few smaller ones, that are continuously sliding past, away from or underneath each other – a process called plate tectonics. The creeping motions of the plates are slow – about as fast as the rate that human fingernails grow – but the forces that come into play as these plates move around are huge. Just look at the great crumpled mountain belts of the Himalayas, formed where the Indian Plate is colliding into the Eurasian Plate; or the deep trenches on the sea floor that form where the Pacific Plate sinks under the Mariana Plate.

## Plate tectonics

Plate tectonics is the current scientific theory that provides an explanation for where, and why, we find volcanoes and earthquakes around the surface of the planet. Since the theory was first developed, in the mid-1960s, it has proved to be very useful in helping to explain many observations that were previously hard to reconcile with each other. Since Planet Earth is more or less a constant size (it is neither growing nor shrinking), the tectonic plates have to move either past, under or over each other. In places where the plates pull apart from each other, hot rock from deep inside the Earth can rise up, melt and form volcanoes; these are often called the 'oceanic ridges'. In places where one plate slides beneath another, huge tectonic forces may cause the overlying plate to buckle, building mountains; and water taken down into the Earth's interior within the sinking plate slowly leaks out, causing the Earth to melt and volcanoes to form at the surface. These regions – where plates are in collision – are called subduction zones, and are often places where there are both huge earthquakes and long chains of active volcanoes, such as around many parts of the Pacific 'Ring of Fire'.

Figure 4    Sampling an active lava flow, Mount Etna, Sicily, 2005. © David M. Pyle.

## Oceanic ridges and continental rifts

The oceanic ridges are actually the longest continuous volcanic mountain-belt system on Earth, stretching for over 40,000 kilometres. Most of the time, volcanism along these ridges goes unnoticed, at it is in the depths of the oceans, but in Iceland, and in a region of north-east Africa called the Afar, some of this ridge system rises above sea level.

The oceanic ridges were first discovered during the laying of the transatlantic telegraph cables in the 1870s, but their importance was only recognized many years later, when scientists looked at the pattern of magnetization in these sea-floor rocks. On a planet with a magnetic field, the pattern of this field can be frozen into the lavas as they erupt and cool. On geological timescales of millions of years, the magnetic field changes in strength, and the 'North' direction wobbles around and may flip orientation completely. By measuring the very small sea-floor magnetic signatures using new naval technology, scientists were able to map the striped 'bar-code' signature of the changing magnetic field through time. In a remarkable discovery in 1963, Fred Vine and Drummond Matthews spotted that this bar-code pattern was symmetrical across the ocean ridges. This magnetic chart recorder requires that most of these sea-floor lavas are erupted in a narrow region at the oceanic ridge, which marks the point of separation between two tectonic plates. These observations led to the now well-established theory that tectonic plates form at oceanic ridges, where magmas from the mantle below rise and freeze to form the trailing edges of the separating plates.

Although these processes are well understood for the sea floor, we still don't have a very good idea of what happens when a continental plate begins to split apart. Imagine pulling at the two ends of a chocolate bar such as a Mars bar. When you start to pull, fractures will form in the brittle chocolate coating. But when does the stretching become concentrated into one big fracture, and where does that fracture form?

To work out how continents break up, geologists have focused their attention on the one place on Earth where this is thought to be happening in the present day: the remote desert region of north-east Africa in the Afar region of Ethiopia and Eritrea. For the past 30 million years this part of the African continent has been stretching, very slowly. The region where the Ethiopian Rift Valley approaches the Red Sea and the Gulf of Aden now forms what is called a 'triple junction', the join where three separate tectonic plates are all moving apart from each other. The join between the Nubian Plate, which lies beneath North Africa, and the Somalian Plate, which forms the north-eastern corner of Africa, is marked by the main Rift Valley. The Arabian Plate has

Figure 5    Lava flows pouring from the new island of Surtsey, on the mid-Atlantic ridge, south of Iceland, 20 April 1964. From Thorarinsson, 1967, *Surtsey, the new island in the North Atlantic*. Photo © Sólarfilma, Iceland.

now pulled just far enough away from the other two plates that the join between the plates is underwater. A part of this evolving plate boundary now lies within the Afar region of Ethiopia. This is an area that is both remote and challenging to work in – it is the hottest inhabited place on Earth, but also a place that is geologically and culturally fascinating. This is the home of the oldest Hominid fossils known, including the 3-million-year-old 'Lucy', and the birthplace of early humans.

A rare opportunity to watch how a continent breaks apart began in late 2005, when a major segment of the plate boundary ruptured. In the space of just a few days, the Dabbahu-Manda-Hararo rift in Afar lurched into life after many hundreds of years of inactivity. The first signs of something unusual were spotted by scientists at the University of Addis Ababa's geophysical observatory, who detected the seismic rattle of moving magma on a distant seismometer. A military helicopter was scrambled, but a fly-by revealed nothing untoward. Two hours later there was a strong earthquake and a dark plume of ash rose high into the sky as a small explosive eruption tore a deep chasm in the flanks of the volcano, Dabbahu. Press reports that suggested a much more dramatic event – with tens of thousands of people displaced and hundreds of goats killed – proved to be exaggerated. It wasn't until a few days later, when satellite radar images were available, that the true drama of the event was revealed. By comparing the shape of the ground surface before and after the eruption, scientists found that a huge fracture had ripped open along a length of 60 kilometres. The eruption site itself was just a very small point at the northern end of the fracture.

The fracture was a new opening in the rift valley. Land on either side of the rift had moved apart by up to 8 metres and sunk (in the middle of the fracture) by up to 3 metres. In just three days the rift had caught up with 250 years of plate pull. But the rift opening didn't leave an open chasm; instead, just below the surface, a large pulse of fresh magma had helped to push the plates apart.

Over the next six years more than a dozen smaller rifting events hit the rift, three of which were accompanied by volcanic 'fire fountains' and flows of basaltic lava. This time around the rift was bristling with newly installed equipment to measure every creak of the rocks, and each of these events was captured in intricate detail. A research aircraft spent five days flying to and fro, photographing and measuring with a laser the surface shape of the rift. Another team of scientists hopped across the rift by helicopter, looking for flat spots to lay out their 100-metre-long lengths of cable so that they could measure tiny electrical currents passing through the Earth's crust to see where pools of molten magma might be hiding at depth.

Since May 2010 the rift has remained silent. It will now remain quiet for the next few centuries, until the next burst of activity and release of pent-up stress caused by the continued movement of the tectonic plates. In Afar the main fracture of the 'Mars bar' formed at least 200,000 years ago, and this has become the place where the trailing edges of the two plates are forming and pulling apart. So here we have a glimpse of the sea-floor spreading process, and the formation of new basaltic crust, identified on land.

## A volcanic arc: Chile

The most visible signs of the link between plate tectonics and volcanism come in the form of the arcuate chains of volcanic peaks that can be traced around the rim of the Pacific Ocean. From southernmost Patagonia to Alaska, from the Aleutians and Japan to the islands of Melanesia and New Zealand, volcanoes dot the landscape with remarkable regularity in 'arcs' that may stretch for many hundreds of kilometres at a time. These include some of the most dangerous and spectacular volcanoes on Earth – from Chimborazo in Ecuador (Figure 6) to Nevado del Ruiz in Colombia, and past the magnificent volcanoes of Agua and Fuego in Guatemala to Mount St Helens in Washington State, USA, and the perfect snow-capped cones of Kliuchevskoy, on Russia's far-eastern island of Kamchatka, and Fuji in Japan.

In these settings volcanism is a consequence of what is called *subduction* – the consumption of one tectonic plate as it sinks deep into the mantle beneath another. In most places where subduction is happening the sinking plate is old and cold, criss-crossed by fractures and steeped in water – immobilized in the structures of low-temperature minerals through the millions of years spent beneath the sea floor. As the cold, wet plate descends it warms up releasing water back into the mantle. Ultimately, this is what causes the Earth to melt in a process that is a little similar to spraying anti-freeze onto ice – the mixture has a lower freezing point, causing the ice to melt. Magmas formed above the sinking slab will then rise because they are buoyant, break their way through the overlying plate and eventually erupt to build the volcanoes of the arc.

The main differences between the sorts of magmas that typically erupt at oceanic ridges and in subduction zones reflect the different ways that the melts form in the first place, and the different pathways that the magmas follow before they reach the surface. Beneath an oceanic ridge, hot rock from the mantle effectively rises up to fill the space created as the plates pull apart. Since the melting temperature of rock increases as you go deeper inside the Earth, allowing

**Toises**

3000 — Volc. de Cotopaxi.

du jour − 0,5 à + 3.°

Neiges perp. a la pente bor. de l'Himalaya (?)

2500 — Temp. moy. 1.°3 cent.

Passage des Andes de l'Assuay.

de jour à + 9.° de nuit 6.° à + 2.°

2000 — Temp. moy. 7.°

Pic de Ténériffe

de jour 5.° 27,5.° de nuit 0.° à n.°

Etna

1500 — Temp. moy. 14,°3.

Passage du Gr.d St. Bernard.

de jour 13.° 15.° 18.° de nuit 9.° 14.°

1000 — Temp. moy. 18.°

de jour 18.° 24.° de nuit 16.° 17.°

Vésuve

500 — Temp. moy. 21,°3.

de jour 18.° 23.° 3.° de nuit 16.° 23.°

Ile de la Puná. Lg. 82° 29'.

T.m 27,5. — Océan pacifique.

Crevasse qui e... d'atteindre la... Term. − 1...

Lecide... nua...

Stereoc. bot.
Bryum. arg. Fied. rup. Gent. rup.
Polytr. jun. Lycopsenia ren. Culcit. ruf.
Calc. niv. Ran. Guen. Hedyot. hypn. Culcit. ledif.
Cænomyce. veen. jul. Collema spong. Sida pich. Geran. ac.
Eudema nubig. Cynan. jul. Melica dact. Aretia and.
Hel. arg. Gyroph. tessel. Deyeux. rigida.
Fest. dacyantha. Sida phyll. Stellar. serpyll.
Pectophyt. ped. Valer. hirt. Racod. rup. ten.
Ramunc. nub. Lycop. crassum. Alchem. rup. Aren. dec.
Lyrip. cc. Carex pich. Arom. lan. Werneria dist.
Myrrh. andic. Fragosa arct. Luzula alp. Gent. diff.
Anchusa pygm. Cerast. imb. Valer. vol. Sticta fidig.
Lupin. sarm. Borrera flac. Eryng. hum. Androm. vol.
Homanth. pinnat. Thym. nubig. Locham. hisp. Buddl. pich.
Mimul. and. Plant. nubigera. Castil. nub. Calceol. niv.
Calceol. eric. Melica scabra. Rubus flor. Ægopog. cenchr. Plantago rig.
Androm. ac. Sibthorpia pich. Alströn. glauc. Escall. berber.
Aster. rup. Festuca and. Senec. nub. Polylep. lanug. Bacch. arb.
Cacal. pat. Polypod. tenuf. Escall. tort. Diplost. lan. Moræa chimb. Spermac. dich.
Poa mulat. Wither. angust. Erod. millefol. Lisit. brom. Solan. aureum.
Swertia brev. Dichond. rep. Besar. grand. Gleichenia revol. Thib. rep.
Calceol. chel. Polypod. ang. Gent. sax. Aral. av. Calceol. flor. Galium inv. Peper. pepl.
Cact. rep. Solan. cald. Stipa emin. Salv. coll. Piper tumid. Ruellia quit.
Piper barb. Panic. aren. Cinchona oval. Eup. rup. Cythar. ilic. Neckera penn.
Ran. trid. Byster. mollis. Paspal. plat. Oreocallis grand.
Mesp. stip. Bacch. hum. Inga insignis. Sed. quit. Calc. lan. Ancistr. arg.
Cheilanth. marg. Lobel. tenera. Pteris sagittata. Lobel. scand. Wedel. bel.
Serieb. pinnat. Cerast. Willd. Hyper. targ. Bidens alaus.
Duranta triac. Tecoma ros. Melast. flor. Pique. art. Rhexia exc. Gaya. can. Gunera scabra.
Cinchona cord. Laplacea spec. Daphne macroph. Salv. lut. Weinm. balb.
Thelyph. pan. Gonzal. tom. Morus cor. Aralia obtusf. Clusia ell. Oval. el.
Escall. pend. Lomaria angust. Lobel. fastig. Lycopod. linifol. Scutell. vol. Cantua pyrif. Camp. ar.
Lycium lox. Loasa loxensis. Lucuma oboo. Tournef. lox. Exostema peruv.
Gnaph. alat. Peristomia oc. Persea sericea. Rhexia conferta. Amar. quit.
Solan. lox. Tillæa rub. Bœhm. ballot. Passifl. manicata. Bœhmeria amp. Croton elegans.
Andromach. verbasc. Cinchona ovalifolia. Persea cinnam. Cactus Bonplandi. Vernon. suav.
Cordia ferruginea. Hæmanth. dub. Eupatorium solidag. Gonzalea tom.
Tacsonia glaberrima. Euphorbia cestrifolia. Cuscuta. foet. Lycium loxense.
Psychotria magnolæf. Mikania angul.
Stachys debilis. Pachyph. distichum. Dendrob. pusillum. Phyllanthus symph. Poa pallida.
Dalechampia hibisc. Salvia macrost. Bœhmeria ampulacea.
Cactus lætus. Setaria cernua. Deyeuxia effusa. Convolvul. abutiloides.
Croton rivinifol. Cinchona caduciflora. Brom. unioloid. Chloris radiata.
Phyllanth. corn. Cenchrus pungens. Clerodendr. molle. Croton abutiloides. Cact. fag.
Paspalum vaginatum. Comyza lyrata. Vitex gigantea. Mertensia pubescens. Cinchona scrobicul.
Priva echinata. Mikan. Tafalli. Cactus nanus. Chloris radiata. Priva echin.
Cecrop. pelt. Chloris radiata. Iatropha urens. Lippia citrodora. Cenchr. pung. Pacourina cirs.
Acacia macr. Mussænda pub. Paspal. conjugat. Acac. Guach. Croton albif.
Inga cand. Anona Bonpl. Lonid. circ. Copp. guay. Conocarp. erecta. Dalech. hib.
Papyr. comosa. Tribul. max. Acac. cochl. Preston. glabr. Adenar. purp.
Cocos nucif. Avicennia tom. Bamb. guad. Cyper. aur. Epidendr. Van. Mach. acum. Croton glandul.
Tournef. cusp. Scirp. oleg. Datura guay.

Ballon de M. Gay-Lussac
le 16 Septembre 1804.

3500

Cime du Chimborazo.

Le Cap. Gerard sur le Tarhi-
-gang. (Himalaya) en 1818.

3000

Pass de Niti Ghaut.
(Himalaya)

2500

M. de Saussure sur la
cime du Montblanc.

Neiges perp. dans les
Andes du Mexique.

Métairie d'Antisana.

2000

Neiges perp. à la pente
mer. de l'Himalaya.

Pic Nethou, plus haute
cime des Pyrenées.

1500

Ville de Quito.

Neiges perp. dans
les Alpes.

Ville d'Alausi.

Ville de Loxa.

1000

Ville de Popayan.

Puy de Dome.

Gualtaquillo.

500
Ville de Caracas.
Plateau du Mysore.

Plateau des Castilles.

Riv. de l'Amazone
à Tomependa.

Grand Para.

of
ues
rochers

commencé à saigner
levres et des gencives.

Lac Yanacoche.

Plaines de Sisgun.

Pl. de Luisa.

Village de Capi.

Yanaurcu
anc. Volcan.

Lg. 8 & 17.

Plateau de Lican.

hot rock from the Earth's mantle to quickly rise will usually cause it to melt spontaneously. The magma that forms in the mantle will be a hot, fluid melt called 'basalt'. In a subduction zone, the presence of water is the main trigger for melting. The magmas that form deep inside the Earth at subduction zones are also basalts, but they may contain rather more water than basalts from other settings. Before they can reach the surface, these basalts have to pass through the cold rocks of the overlying plate, causing them to cool and crystallize. The end result is that not much basalt makes it to the surface in subduction zones, and those magmas that do may be more crystal-rich and be significantly less fluid than basalt. As a result, the sorts of magmas erupted at arc volcanoes include 'andesites' and 'rhyolites', and where the magmas are both viscous and water-rich, they may often erupt with great violence.

One of the best places to get a glimpse of the scale of this process is southern Chile, where the volcanic chain of the 'southern Andean volcanic zone' stretches for over 1,000 kilometres south from Santiago. This is where my passion for volcanoes was first kindled as a child, during the turbulent year of 1971/2. I vividly remember a summer holiday camping in the Chilean Lake District to a backdrop of steaming and snow-capped volcanoes. The lakes, I now know, have all formed within the past 18,000 years – filling valleys that were dammed by the debris of retreating glaciers that had once buried the region under a kilometre or more of ice. One of these volcanoes, Villarrica, had just recently erupted. Somewhere in a family photo album there's a fading picture of me sitting on the gravelly edge of a very recent volcanic mudflow.

Thirty years later I took the mid-morning flight south from Santiago towards Puerto Montt, and was fortunate to get a window seat on the left-hand side of the plane on a wonderfully clear day. The vista, once any early morning cloud has cleared, is almost unbeatable as you fly along the length of one of the most spectacular chains of young and active volcanoes in the world. Here, the snow- and ice-capped volcanoes pop up out of the landscape every 50–70 kilometres. Many, though not all, are immediately recognizable as volcanoes from their conical shape and their summit craters. They are often in pairs, either as distinct but closely spaced mountains (Tolhuaca and Lonquimay) or as 'twin peaks' forming the summit of an elongated massif (Llaima, Mocho-Choshuenco). Many of the volcanoes are very young structures, with well-formed cones that can only have formed after the end of the last major glaciation in the region. These cones often perch within the much larger craters formed earlier in the history of the ancient volcano. The accessibility of the volcanoes of the Southern Volcanic Zone of the Andes makes this a wonderful place to study volcanic processes and volcano behaviour, and at least four of these volcanoes have erupted in recent years.

Figure 6 *previous page* Chimborazo, Ecuador – the world's tallest stratovolcano. Alexander von Humboldt attempted the climb on 25 June 1802, making many observations on the way up. From Humboldt's *Voyage aux régions équinoxiales du nouveau continent…* 1810. Oxford, Bodleian Library, 20910 a.2.

Villarrica (or 'Ruka Pillan' in the language of Mapudungun) is one of the most active volcanoes of southern Chile and is a popular tourist destination in the heart of the Chilean Lake District. Written records of past eruptions begin in 1558, shortly after the original founding of the town of Villa Rica. More complete records of past eruptions can be pieced together from studies of the ash layers trapped in the muddy sediments at the bottom of the nearby glacial lake Villarrica. The volcano Villarrica has been in a continuous state of agitation since the last eruption in 1984–85, with a small pond of fuming lava often visible within the summit crater. After a four-hour trudge up the increasingly steep snowcap there are breathtaking views of the Chilean Lake District from the summit, as well as of the neighbouring volcanoes from Osorno to Llaima, and waves of fumes and showers of delicate golden magma foam from the crater. Almost as exhilarating is the descent, a mad 15-minute controlled slide to the edge of the ice cap.

In early 2015, Villarrica began to show signs of increased unrest, with more seismicity and visible activity in the summit crater (Figure 7). Eruptions in 1963–64 and 1971 were characterized by vigorous 'Strombolian' explosions from the summit, with short paroxysms of fire fountaining followed by the formation of lava flows. The major hazards at Villarrica come from lahars, or wet mudflows, which form when snow and ice from the summit glacier are rapidly melted by contact with hot magma. In 1963 and 1971 the lahars that swept off the volcano caused considerable damage and many casualties in towns and villages around the volcano. Today, the summit of Villarrica is covered by about a cubic kilometre of ice, equivalent to a body of water three times larger than Windermere.

The 2015 eruption of Villarrica wasn't unexpected, but began very quickly, early in the morning on 3 March. For about 30 minutes, the flanks of the volcano were lit up by the spectacular paroxysm, a column of red-hot ejecta that could be seen from many kilometres away and that provided spectacular uplighting of the convecting ash and steam clouds forming above the volcano. The paroxysm released a large puff of ash that rose to about 9 kilometres above sea level and could be seen from weather satellites, and a burp of volcanic sulphur dioxide gas that was also visible from space. The eruption coated the summit of Villarrica with a fresh layer of dark grey volcanic 'spatter', and small amounts of volcanic ash were washed down the local drainages and into Lake Villarrica.

A little over a month later, and 200 kilometres further south, the volcano Calbuco burst into eruption in the late afternoon of 22 April. Unlike its photogenic neighbour, Osorno, Calbuco is a complex and rugged volcano with a complicated but poorly known history. The little that we do know about Calbuco's backstory comes from historical records, which suggest that it has had

Figure 7    Villarrica in violent eruption, March 2015. A 'Strombolian' fire fountain from the summit crater of Villarrica creates a large ash plume. Note the lightning, which is a common feature of explosive eruptions. © Francisco Negroni / Alamy.

repeated eruptions since the late nineteenth century. Its most spectacular recent eruption was in February 1961, which threw up an ash plume 12 to 15 kilometres high, just a few months after the world's largest recorded earthquake had struck the region. After 1961, Calbuco was almost completely quiet, apart from a small eruption that lasted for four hours on 26 August 1972 and some strong gas emissions in August 1996.

The eruptions of 22–23 April began with no real warning, and sent strong, buoyant plumes of volcanic ash high into the atmosphere (Figure 8). The first part of the eruption lasted 90 minutes, sent an ash column to 16 kilometres and ejected 40 million cubic metres of ash, enough to half-fill Wembley stadium. After a six-hour pause, the second part of the eruption sent an ash column to 17 kilometres and emptied 170 million cubic metres of ash across northern Patagonia. The eruption was accompanied by dramatic pulses of lightning and was easily visible from space. Several thousand people were temporarily evacuated, and nearby towns, villages and lakes were badly affected by thick pumice, ash deposits and lahars. For the next five days, the ash clouds swirled across southern Chile and Argentina, passing over an area of over 400,000 square kilometres, disrupting air travel across southern South America and indirectly affecting at least 4 million people. Ash fell from Concepción, on Chile's Pacific coast, to Trelew and Puerto Madryn on the Atlantic coast of Argentina. After a week, activity died down and Calbuco slowly settled back into repose.

## Measuring volcanoes

Two short pieces of explanation are needed: how geologists classify eruptions and how they measure eruptions.

Volcanoes come in all sorts of shapes and sizes – from the great, flooded craters of Santorini (Greece), Toba (Indonesia) and Krakatoa (Indonesia) and the grand massifs of Mauna Loa (Hawaii) and Kilimanjaro (Tanzania) to the archetypical snow-capped cones of Fuji (Japan), Cotopaxi (Ecuador) and Villarrica (Chile). Each of these sorts of volcanoes is the product of many eruptions over many thousands or tens of thousands of years. There are also small volcanoes, the sort that pop up as pimples in volcanic fields or stretch out in lines, tracing the path of a once magma-filled fracture at depth. Some of these may only erupt once, before sealing up and falling prey to the slow ravages of erosion and weathering.

Eruptions also come in a variety of shapes and sizes – sometimes violently explosive, shooting vast ash-laden plumes high into the atmosphere; other times, bubbling steadily in a simmering cauldron of lava. In explosive eruptions, rock fragments – usually pumice or ash – may be either deposited to the ground by falling, with gravity, from an ash plume that might be many kilometres high in the atmosphere, or deposited from violent hot avalanches that have cascaded off the sides of the volcano. These hot avalanches have attracted a host of different names, depending on the nature of the current (if observed) or the deposit, from 'nuée ardente', or 'block and ash flow', to 'pyroclastic flow' and 'pyroclastic surge'. To the geologist, the deposits formed by these different processes look very different: 'fallout' deposits tend to have many fragments of the same size, having effectively been sorted in the atmosphere; while 'flow' deposits tend to be much more variable or heterogeneous in particle size and in the way that the deposits appear in the field.

Volcanic eruptions that we know of span an extraordinary range of sizes – from the few cubic metres of lava that might dribble out of a vent on the bizarre 'washing soda' volcano of Oldoinyo Lengai (Tanzania) to the thousands of cubic kilometres of pulverized magma disgorged during the great eruptions of Toba 75,000 years ago, or of the La Garita crater in Colorado 29 million years ago. Eruptions may be short – from the few minutes of a violent steam explosion, such as the fatal eruption of Mount Ontake, Japan, in 2014 – or last for generations – as in the current eruptions of the Soufrière Hills Volcano, Montserrat (began in 1995), Kilauea, Hawaii (began in 1983), or Stromboli (puffing persistently since records began over 2,000 years ago). To capture some of this, volcano scientists tend to use short-hand terms to describe typical eruption styles: 'Hawaiian' – meaning lava flows and occasional fire fountains; 'Strombolian' – intermittent, small to moderate bubble bursts and explosions; and 'Plinian' – violently explosive and ash cloud-forming eruptions. With the exception of Plinian, which was named for Pliny the Elder (see Chapter 1), these names usually describe the typical state of an exemplar volcano.

To measure the size of explosive eruptions, volcano scientists often use a simple numerical scale called the volcanic explosivity index. This is a little bit like the Richter scale for earthquakes – so an eruption that rates five on this index is about ten times larger than an eruption that rates four on the index. On this index, the largest eruption of the past ten years is about five (Puyehue, Chile, in 2011); the largest eruption of the past hundred years rates six (Pinatubo, Philippines, in 1991); and the largest eruptions ever known have a rating of eight (for example, Toba, Indonesia, 74,000 years ago, and Yellowstone, USA, 640,000 years ago).

Figure 8    Calbuco volcano, Chile, in eruption on the evening of 22 April 2015. A vertical eruption plume is forming a broad and spreading umbrella cloud of ash, about 16 kilometres high. Winds carried this ash cloud, which spread across Argentina and then around the world over the next few days. © epa European Pressphoto Agency / Alamy.

Figure 9 *overleaf* Volcanic activity in the central cone of Vesuvius before the great eruption of 1767, showing mild Strombolian activity at the summit and lava flows around the base of the cone. From William Hamilton's *Campi Phlegraei*, 1776. Oxford, Bodleian Library, Vet. F5 b.2, plate 9.

# CHAPTER 1
## Volcanoes in early accounts

H UMANS HAVE LIVED with and around volcanoes for millions of years. More than 2 million years ago, early humans in the great Rift Valley of Ethiopia were using volcanic rocks – lumps of glassy obsidian and dense, strong and finely crystalline basalt – to make tools for chopping and cutting. Perhaps as long ago as 36,000 years, our prehistoric ancestors were decorating their caves with fountains of red droplets to mark the eruption of a nearby volcanic cone. Certainly by about 9,000 years ago, residents of the Neolithic town of Çatalhöyük in Turkey had fashioned a mural of their neighbourhood in one of the houses which included an image thought to represent the young volcano of Hasan Daği, which lies just a few kilometres away. Across the world, volcanic materials, ancient and modern, are used in construction and painting, and myths, legends and stories as deep as time tell and retell oral histories of great eruptions of the past and of volcanic disasters and their human consequences. Some of these stories have made it on to paper; others are yet to be recorded.

The oldest writings known that record volcanic activity of the past come from the Mediterranean, and the Greek philosophers, who knew of the volcanoes of southern Italy and the Tyrrhenian and Aegean seas. By the sixth century BCE, Heraclitus, Pythagoras and Anaxagoras had all helped to develop ideas of a central fire within Earth which caused winds, earthquakes and volcanic eruptions. Empedocles, who lived near Mount Etna, sought to explain the properties of known materials by mixing fire, earth, air and water in different amounts. He supposed that the interior of the Earth was molten, and that lava formed when this molten material rose to the surface. According to legend 'Great Empedocles, that ardent soul, leapt into Etna, and was roasted whole'.[2] In the fourth century BCE, Aristotle refined ideas about the nature of volcanic activity, developing ideas about the way that fires within the Earth would act on trapped

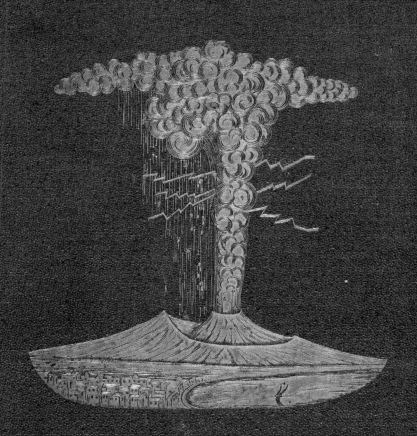

ERUPTION OF VESUVIUS

AS SEEN FROM NAPLES    OCTOBER.1822.

moisture and air, leading to winds, tremors and throbbings in the same way that might happen in the human body. The associations of volcanic eruptions with wind and fire, and ways of thinking about what might be happening in the deep, inaccessible interior, remain strong themes in ways that people write and think about volcanoes.

Greek and Roman poets and historians wrote widely of their impressions and experiences of volcanic activity. Virgil's *Aeneid* describes how Aeneas came to visit the priestess Sybil, in a cave near Avernus in the steamy and sulphurous Campi Flegrei, otherwise known as the Phlegrean Fields. Together, they crossed the river Styx in search of the underworld. Dramatic eruptions of Etna in 122 BCE and 44 BCE certainly influenced contemporary writers such as Virgil and, later, Ovid, who described it 'glowing with its sulphurous furnaces'.[3]

Perhaps the best-known, and clearest, description of a volcanic eruption and its dramatic consequences come from the letters of Pliny the Younger, following the eruption of Vesuvius on 24 August in 79 CE. At the time, Pliny the Younger was seventeen years old. His uncle, Pliny the Elder, was a statesman and polymath who had written an encyclopaedic work on natural history. At the time of the eruption, Pliny the Elder was a commander in the Roman Navy and stationed at Misenum (Miseno), a port in the Bay of Naples close to the Phlegrean Fields.

In the early afternoon on 24 August, they noticed an unusually sized cloud that appeared to be rising from a nearby mountain. It looked a little like a typical Mediterranean pine tree, 'for it rose to a great height on a sort of trunk and then split off into branches'.[4] Pliny the Elder set sail to investigate and, realizing the scale of what was happening, commanded the fleet to head for the affected coast to provide assistance.

The activity gradually escalated: 'Ashes were already falling, hotter and thicker as the ships drew near the coast, followed by bits of pumice and blackened stones: then suddenly they were in shallow water, and the shore was blocked by the debris from the mountain.'[5]

The eruption continued overnight with 'broad sheets of fire and leaping flames' blazing at several points on Mount Vesuvius. By the next morning, 'buildings [were] now shaking with violent shocks, and seemed to be swaying to and fro, as if they were torn from their foundations. Outside there was the danger of falling pumice-stones, even though these were light and porous'.[6] To protect themselves from falling ejecta,

Figure 11 Detail from the front board of Scrope's *Considerations on Volcanoes*, 1825. Oxford, Bodleian Library, (OC) 188 e.28.

people tied pillows to their heads with cloths. Pliny the Elder was overcome, perhaps by the ashy fumes, and died shortly after.

In a later letter, Pliny explained the context: 'For several days past there had been earth tremors which were not particularly alarming … but that night the shocks were so violent that everything felt as if it were not only shaken but overturned.'[7] He later described the descent of the violent ash-rich pyroclastic clouds that 'sank down to earth and covered the sea; blotting out Capri and hiding the promontory of Misenum from sight'.[8] He continued:

> I looked round: a dense black cloud was coming up behind us,
> spreading over the earth like a flood. We had scarcely sat down to rest
> when darkness fell, not the dark of a moonless or cloudy night, but as if
> the lamp had been put out in a closed room. You could hear the shrieks
> of women, the wailing of infants, and the shouting of men; some were
> calling their parents, others their children or their wives, trying to
> recognize them by their voices. People bewailed their own fate, and
> there were some who prayed for death in their terror of dying.[9]
> …
> At last the darkness thinned and dispersed into smoke or cloud;
> then there was genuine daylight, and the sun actually shone out, but
> yellowish as it is during an eclipse. We were terrified to see everything
> changed, buried deep in ashes like snowdrifts.[10]

Figure 12   Fragment of a carbonized papyrus scroll from the library of a private house in Herculaneum that was buried in the 79 CE eruption of Vesuvius. The scrolls were presented to the Bodleian Library in 1810 by George, Prince of Wales. Oxford, Bodleian Library, MS. Gr. class. b. 1 (P)/1 detail.

This phenomenon, captured in amazing detail by Pliny, is one of the most damaging and destructive ways that volcanoes erupt. Pyroclastic density currents behave a little like hot avalanches of rock and ash. At Vesuvius, it was the erupting column of ash and pumice that collapsed, spreading rapidly across the countryside, burying towns and villages under tens of metres of hot, choking debris as it went. Similar phenomena can also happen when parts of volcanoes collapse under their own weight, or when violent explosions are triggered when magma hits a body of water during an eruption. Non-volcanic examples of similar phenomena include the violent blast waves that were first seen during the ground-level nuclear bomb tests of the 1950s and 1960s, or the toxic

Frag. 3.

Frag. 6 e 7.

1.

Frag. 2.

Frag. 4.

Frag. 5.

Frag. 8.

Frag. 10.

Frag. 11.

Papiro N: 118.

dust clouds that poured through Manhattan after the Twin Towers collapsed on 9/11.

The eruption of Vesuvius in 79 CE remains an iconic event, in part because a dramatic eyewitness account of the events has been preserved, but also because the cities that were inundated by pyroclastic debris during the eruption – Pompeii and Herculaneum – have now been rediscovered. This has allowed forensic studies of the geological story of what happened to be compared directly to written histories, in a way that is rarely possible.

After August 79 CE, we know little of the detail of Vesuvius's behaviour. This huge eruption reshaped the face of the volcano, carving a great crater in what had previously been the conical summit or 'Somma' of Vesuvius. Careful detective work over the years has started to fill in some of the gaps. It seems likely that the 79 CE eruption may have been followed by some decades to centuries of lava flow and fire-fountaining eruptions, helping to build a new 'Gran Cono del Vesuvio' within the collapse crater. A large explosive eruption shook the volcano again in 512 CE, and an extended period of quiet – perhaps as long as 500 years – preceded the onset of the next explosive phase, which began violently in December 1631.

## Hades

Where did the idea of the '*descent* to Hades' come from? Most volcanoes whose craters I have peered into have required hours of limb-sapping toil to ascend. This has involved scrambling through scree, scoria and snow to peer over the punctured summit into the fuming crater below, followed moments later by grasping for the gas mask before the fume triggers an asthmatic response.

Of course, Hades never was modelled on a volcanic *mountain*. With Vulcano, Vesuvius, Etna and Stromboli nearby, these live volcanoes and their pyrotechnic feats provided plenty of material to residents and passers-by, who dreamt up stories of angry gods, deep hearths, thunderclaps and lightning. Instead, Hades was modelled on the slumbering, restless caldera of Campi Flegrei (Figure 13). Today, this is a vast steaming volcanic playground of fuming mudpots and steaming sulphur pits, a landscape that is alien from wherever on Earth you may have arrived. Here, the clues to the mysterious, restless depths of the planet are tantalizing. Elegant columns, fragments of a great

Figure 13    The Temple of Serapis (in the Campi Flegrei region), now thought to be the Roman marketplace, Pozzuoli, in the Phlegrean Fields in 1810. Borings on the columns show how the land surface has sunk below sea level and then risen up again due to the movements of magma at depth. *Elogio di Francesco de' Marchi*, by Francesco Tognetti, 1819. Oxford, Bodleian Library, 3 DELTA 311 (1), figure 5.

Roman marketplace, show the unmistakable tidemarks of marine borings two or three metres above the present-day shoreline – sure signs of the rhythmic ups and downs experienced by this great volcanic system over past millennia. Here you may find the Elysian Fields, the rivers Phlegethon and Styx and Lake Avernus, the entrance to Hades.

Campi Flegrei remains an active volcanic system. In 1538, Monte Nuovo, the new mountain, appeared rapidly, followed nearly a century later by the brisk re-awakening of Vesuvius in December 1631. But how, without following Aeneas, can we understand the deeper workings of the inferno? And why are these hot mountains so often associated with water? Volcanologists are historians of the magmatic world; we can never *know* what is about to happen, but instead build our understanding of what may happen from careful retrospective analysis of the archives of the material world. From these dusty fragments of past eruptions, and from the delicate marginalia preserved in mineral form, we learn to read the stories of past eruptions and of what went before.

The only eruption of the historical period in the Campi Flegrei (Figure 14) was the short-lived but violent eruption that formed the 'new mountain', Monte Nuovo. Several descriptions of this eruption survive, reproduced in translation in Sir William Hamilton's *Campi Phlegraei*.

One was provided by Marco Antonio delli Falconi, a priest, who later became bishop of Cariati in Calabria:

> For two years there have been frequent earthquakes at Pozzuolo, at Naples, and the neighbouring parts. On the day and the night before the appearance of this eruption about twenty shocks great and small were felt. The eruption made its appearance the 29th September 1538; it was on a Sunday, about an hour in the night, and they began to see flames of fire fixing in the little valley that lies between the Monte Barbaro and the hillock called del Pericolo, the road to the lake of Avernus. In a short time, the fire increased to such a degree that it burst open the earth and threw up so great a quantity of ash and pumice-stones mixed with water as covered the whole country. This continued two days and nights, when the smoke and force of the fire began to ease. The fourth day at 22 o'clock, there was so great an eruption, that I

was not far from Misenum and saw many columns of smoke shoot up with the most terrible noise I ever heard. Later, people reported that the eruption had thrown up a mountain in that valley, not less than three miles in circumference and almost as high as the Monte Barbaro. A thing almost incredible, that in such a short time so considerable a mountain could have been formed.

On its summit there is a mouth in the form of a cup, which may be a quarter of a mile in circumference, from which there issues a constant smoke. The Sunday following, the 6th October, many people going to see this phenomenon and some having ascended the mountain, there happened so sudden and horrid an eruption with so great a smoke that many of these people were stifled, some of which could never be found. The number of dead or lost amounted to twenty four.[11]

Tragically, this is a pattern of calamity that is still seen at volcanoes today. There are repeated examples of people being seriously injured or killed in eruptions that occur days, weeks or months after the activity first started. In many cases, people may be attempting to return home to collect belongings or tend to livestock. But there are examples of volcano sightseers, perhaps wanting to use an apparent lull in activity to get in close and see at first hand the consequences of a volcanic eruption. One of the worst recent examples of this was in June 1991 at Mount Unzen, Japan. Unzen had been erupting since May 1991 after a series of small explosions beginning six months earlier. Volcanologists and film-makers Maurice and Katia Krafft led a group, including journalists and fire fighters, deep into the evacuated zone, where they were caught unawares by a larger than expected hot avalanche of volcanic debris. All forty-three people in the group died.

## Volcanoes of the Atlantic Ocean

Beyond the volcanoes of classical Italy – Vesuvius, Stromboli, Vulcano and Etna – all of which were well known to the ancients, volcanoes in other locations were described and sketched in reports from early travellers.

Figure 14 The Bay of
Naples, showing the
steaming lakes, vents and
craters of the Campi Flegrei.
From the Grand Tour guide,
*Voyage pittoresque...* by J.C.
Richard de Saint-Non, 1782.
Oxford, Bodleian Library,
Arch.Antiq. B III.12.

CARTE DU GOLFE DE POUZZOLES AVEC UNE PARTIE DES CHAMPS PHLÉGRÉENS DANS LA TERRE DE LABOUR

St Brendan, an Irish monk in the sixth century, wrote an epic tale of a voyage to the Promised Land that saw him setting sail across the north Atlantic. Over the course of several years, Brendan and his travelling companions encountered wild seas, rare beasts and untamed islands – two of which were certainly volcanoes (Figure 15): 'They came within view of an island which was rugged and rocky, covered with slag, without trees or grass but full of forges. As they passed by, a savage rushed to the shore, carrying tongs with a burning mass of slag of great size and intense heat.'[12]

On another day, they witnessed 'a large and high mountain in the ocean … with cliffs that were so high they could scarcely see the top, that were black as coal and upright like a wall'.[13] The mountain had 'a great smoke issuing from its summit', as they departed the peak of the mountain came free from the clouds and the sailors could see 'flames shooting up into the sky … so that the mountain seemed a burning pyre'. Many medieval manuscripts of the voyage are in existence, and one of these in the Bodleian collection has a delightful marginal sketch of the volcano – quite possibly one of the oldest manuscript sketches of a volcano in existence. From the descriptions, these certainly sound like volcanoes, but whether they are volcanoes in the north Atlantic – perhaps Iceland or Jan Mayen – or further south – perhaps the Azores or the Canary islands – remains unknown.

## The Mediterranean

The early Renaissance period saw a growth in books on travel, geography and history that described voyages and journeys, or sought to describe the world around us. In the early fifteenth century, Cristoforo Buondelmonti, a Venetian monk, wrote a wonderfully illustrated guide to the islands of Greece, the *Liber insularum archipelagi*. Several manuscript versions of this book exist, written in Latin and with vivid sketches of many of the islands of the Aegean and central Mediterranean, including the volcanic islands of Santorini and Nisyros (Figures 16, 73).

Santorini, a splendid crescent-shaped island, was dormant at this time, not having erupted since about the eighth century (Chapter 7). Nisyros is a classical 'stratovolcano' that rises out of the sea between the Greek island of Kos and the Datça peninsula of Turkey. Although it is a small island, it certainly has the appearance of a volcano, with

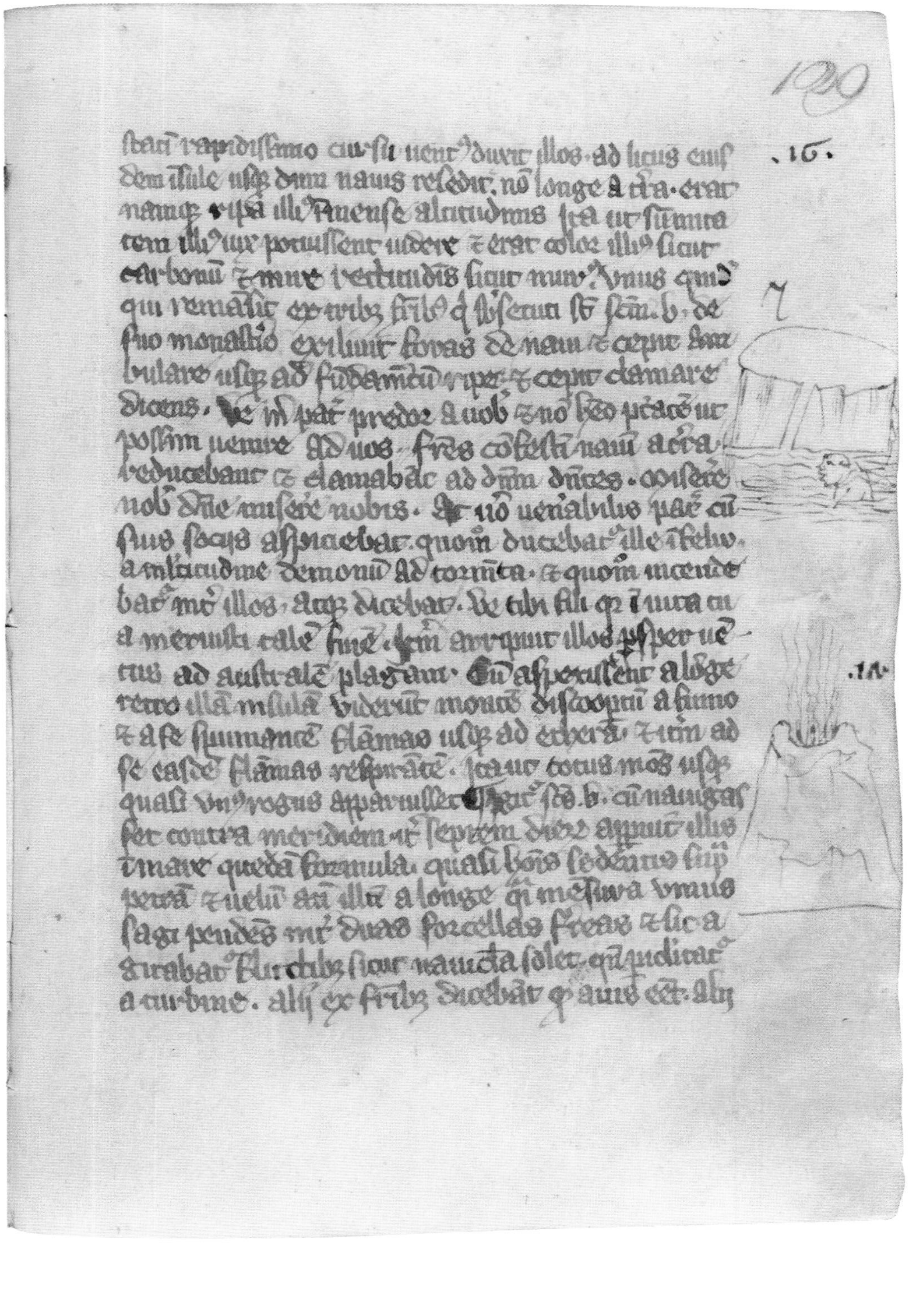

Figure 15 Sketch of a volcano in the north Atlantic, from an early fifteenth-century life of St Brendan. Oxford, Bodleian Library, MS. Laud Misc. 173, fol. 129r.

Caria
Nisaros
Ethensmos

Scendi situm episcopis nunc ad carias
hodie nisaros in ciuitate valenn cum
etheo monte. caria de grece nunc latine in
grece latine insula interpretatur. hic flau
us consul rediens de gibus orientis z acc
pugnaturus contre gallos urgunatur e
uictoriam obtinere z sic rem in luce vsolu

Flaminius gsul
Cleopatra
Antonius

Itaq insula hec beniuola romanis h abeta
phanc etiam transiens cleopatre cum nor
nio z nolentes ciues preceptis eoz obedi
totam insula deleuere z xviij circuitu
z quinq uidentur oppida: quoz duo pncipa
hioros Mandrachi z palechastro z pnca
nichi in dea, z argos sunt in circuitu ci
medium mons erigitur altissimus: cuiu
summitate p Etreneneos mentus sulfurei ig
die ac nocte eructat in altum: ut insola
scopuli apud liparum uidentur. in desce
uo montis ad ictum lapidis calidissimus
emanat in unu z iuplino circa lacum
prundissimum q obscurum aque defcodu
ibiq colentes q btrate maxim sulfuris uide
toribus preparare z quia intrta uigi in
uas caloris demedio usq ad iuctice im iq
ert autus sunt scbulazq accedere ligneu
Et z n. hic tanta fecunditas piscium: q
ui anno houerentur naues que. Ad coniu
pod montes contigua maris spelunche c
sistit: ad quam circumstantes doloub oppil
cedunt z diu morati in patriam incolum
reuertuntur. Et q cō cana ut psiunt ba
insula habetur sepe z sepius tot z enta
renta uibiq repunt q fontes ob hoc p
locum uiro male ducentes reliquunt z pcu

accedere uoluendum. colentes suo tale est ter
mineum quibilo hinc: q̃ in eo no additure
curaure;

INSVLA FARIE

Vne ad amphaleam olim hodie Scarapela
meum ypombo aulum q̃ in air plinius̃
Amphalea libere ciuitatis er uibus octuagista
nouem milia passuum q̃ in sup ouidius,
Hinc anaphea mingit er infinit i stiphaleares̃
Promisit anaphea rede q̃ stiphalea bello:
E inctae q̃ piscosu in sp. uadis; inuudo inter re
mississima. er i i so uenis ampla in qbus plurima
uontra delolata uidentur Ad honer nat si oppidu
admeridiem q̃ occidum ciuitas apparet Stimpa
lea d õn. Sunt er eis q insulam uigintelale
quoqz oppidozum er hinc uede y ciuitius poti opti
mi uoludmtur er delolati iam diu apinatissime

Stimphale
Scarapela

Vathi
Stimphalea

Figure 16   The active
volcano on the island of
Nisyros, Greece. From
Cristoforo Buondelmonti's
*Liber insularum archipelagi*,
c. 1420, in a copy dated 1474.
Oxford, Bodleian Library,
MS. Canon. Misc. 280, fols.
19v–20r.

steep sides that scoop down to the sea and enclose an impressive crater that occupies much of the interior of the island. The volcanic history of the island has proved hard to unravel, but for the past thirty years it has been the most restless volcano in the Aegean Sea. Anyone who has made the steep descent onto the barren central plain, walked across the brilliant white dust of the dried-out lake floor underfoot and choked on the steamy fumes rising from the boiling puddles and hissing mud pits in the Stefanos and Polyvotis craters will attest to its volcanic nature.

Buondelmonti, who was probably writing in about 1420 CE, vividly describes a high mountain in the centre of the island 'which day and night poured out sulphurous fires from subterranean pathways, as at Stromboli island near Lipari'.[14] Nearby, he described a hot spring, discharging into a deep lake, where the inhabitants would collect large quantities of sulphur to sell to passing merchants. One of the craters, perched on the flanks of Nisyros's tallest peak, is known as Phlegethon – a reference to the fiery river of the underworld. Cristoforo Buondelmonti's description is the only published record of volcanic activity at Nisyros until the 1830s. This poses the usual challenge to volcano scientists: was the activity in 1420 unusual in anyway? Or was Buondelmonti simply describing the sorts of activity that one might see at the volcano today, using language that wouldn't seem out of place in a tourist brochure or travel blog?

Nisyros last erupted in the late nineteenth century, in a sequence of violent steam and mud explosions that excavated several small explosion craters in the centre of the island. These were most likely eruptions caused by changes in the hot, acidic waters that are circulating just under the surface. Many volcanoes are thought to have 'hydrothermal systems' such as that at Nisyros, fed either by surface waters or seawater and heated and acidified by deep hot sources of magma and leaking gas.

## The sixteenth century

By the sixteenth century, the invention of the printing press had opened up new possibilities for sharing information widely. One of the earliest of the printed encyclopaedias was Sebastian Münster's *Cosmographiae universalis* (Figure 17). Sebastian Münster was a German cartographer and scholar. The first version of his

Figure 17  Woodcut of Mount Etna volcano accompanying a description of activity on Tenerife. Sebastian Münster, *Cosmographiae universalis*, 1550. Oxford, Bodleian Library, Antiq.c.GS.1550.2, p.1113

religione & timore Dei, sed successu temporum ad Christum sunt reducti, maxime quatuor insulæ. Aiunt singulas propriam habere linguam. Teneriffa & Gran canaria, id est grandis Canaria, sunt cæteris maiores. Teneriffa uideri potest à longe quinquaginta milliariorum Germanicorum interuallo, quando cœlum est serenum, idq ob hanc causam. Consurgit in medio insulæ petra quædã fortissima & maxima, quæ quindecim leucis putatur erigi in altum expuitq perpetuo ignem haud secus quàm Aetna in Sicilia. Viuunt incolæ pane hordeaceo, carnibus & lacte. Abundant autem capris, onagris & sicubus. Carent uino & tritico.

# LIBER SEXTVS
## Cosmographiæ, per Sebastianum Munsterum
ex probatis autoribus & scriptoribus, antiquis & recentioribus collectus & in unum conflatus.

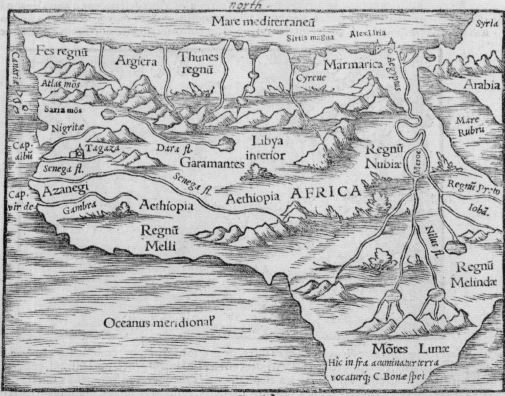

*Cosmographiae* was published in German in 1544, and was quickly followed by versions in Latin (1550), French (1552) and Italian (1558). Part of its success can be attributed to the many and wonderful woodcuts of maps, people and places used throughout to illustrate the volume. Münster writes of the 'mountains of perpetual fire, that burst out with great violence, throwing out cinders, sands, sulphur, pumices and stones that have the appearance of iron',[15] of which Etna is a prime example. He also describes the volcano of Tenerife in the Canary Islands and its 'perpetual fires like Etna in Sicily'.[16] This is a reference to an eruption from the rift zone that stretches north-west from the central peak of Pico del Teide volcano that is reported to have been seen in August 1492 by Christopher Columbus. Delightful as they are, none of the volcano illustrations in *Cosmographiae* are anything other than vignettes of imagined mountains throwing out smoke, flames and stones, with or without a walled city at its feet.

Another volcano that was well known at this time was Hekla, in Iceland, which 'from time to time throws out huge rocks, sulphur, and cinders over great distances'.[17] During the historical period that Iceland has been inhabited, since about 900 CE, Hekla (Figure 18) has been one of the most active volcanoes in the northern Atlantic. The first major historical eruption of Hekla, in 1104 CE, was also one of its largest – rating a score of five on the volcanic explosivity index and depositing a major pumice blanket called H1 across half of Iceland, with extensive lava flows down the flanks of the volcano. Since then, Hekla has erupted another twenty-two times, most recently in the year 2000.

Hekla features prominently in other early maps and accounts of volcanoes, and descriptions of Iceland. Magnus Olaus's wonderful woodcut from 1555 (Figure 18) shows Mons Hekla stoked by flames from below, along with two neighbouring snow-capped volcanoes – Mons Crucis and another unnamed volcano. Ortelius's splendid map of Iceland from 1585 (see Figure 39) features a dramatically fiery Hekla, 'perpetually condemned to storms and snow, vomits stones with terrible noise', and neighbouring ice-capped volcanoes of Myrdalsjökull, home to Katla volcano, Solheimajökull and Eyjafjallajökull – which, of course, erupted with major consequences for northern Europe in April 2010.

Figure 18   Woodcut image of Hekla volcano, Iceland, flanked by snow-capped mountains and fed by fires from below. From Magnus Olaus, *Historiæ de gentibus septentrionalibus*, 1555. Oxford, Bodleian Library, Toynbee 1152, p.33.

# OLAI MAGNI GOTHI
## ARCHIEPISCOPI VPSALENSIS
### DE MIRA NATVRA RERVM
#### Septentrionalium.

### EPITOME LIBRI SECVNDI.

*De venis sulfureis, & combustione aquarum.*
#### Cap. I.

S Vnt quædā sulphureæ venæ riuis aquarum vicinæ, quæ plerunque accensæ la-
tius, in modum flammarum, cuncta in
circuitu depopulaturæ vagantur. Quod
spectaculum in Islandia, & Scotia, terris
frigidissimis, continuo ardoris incremē-
to habitatores intuentur. Præterea in Meridionali Go-
thia, non procul à ciuitate Vexionensi, campestris &
limosus lacus est, qui ignea sua virtute, quodcunque
coctile in eo dimissum chordáque extractū, quasi mo-
mentaneo vel exiguo temporis momento, coctum vel
adustum remittit. Hancque naturam, lacum similem,
prope metropolim Nidrosiensem regni Noruegiæ, habere compertum est, eo præcipuè argumento, quod in
medijs frigoribus nunquam congelatur.

*De quorundam montium admirabili natura.*
#### Cap. 2.

IN Islandia qualis naturæ montes sint, iā arbitror fe-
rè toti mundo compertū: eò quòd vltra veterum re-
lationem,

lationem, in charta nostra Gothica descriptionem
Ptolæmæi supplendo, horum mōtium situm, & naturam osten limus esse singularem, scilicet in eorum vertice niuem fore quasi perpetuam, & in base ignem sul-
phureum continuè sine sui consumptione exardescen-
tem. Qui propius accedunt, vi pulueris & fauillæ sca-
turientis facilè suffocantur, & maximè cùm in multis
locis, torridæ voragines cum cinere apparent montium
combustorū & vallium : quæ iterum tacitis incremen-
tis sulphureis succrescentibus, quasi circulari temporum spatio disponuntur ad combustionem. Sunt etiam
intra Noruegiē limites vastissimi, altissimíque montes:
quatuor dietarum ascensuros, totidémque è vertice
descensuros admittentes.

*Islandiæ & eius gentis descriptio.* Cap. 3.

ISlandia terra est subiecta polo Arctico, vento præ-
sertim Circio opposita, ac mari Glaciali propinqua,
C          atque

ATHANASII KIRCHERI
E Soc. JESU

# MUNDUS
# SUBTERRANEUS,

### in XII Libros digestus;

*Douce*
*R. ## 149.*

QUO

**Divinum Subterrestris Mundi Opificium, mira**
Ergasteriorum Naturæ in eo distributio, verbo παυδάμορφον
Protei Regnum,

*Universæ denique Naturæ majestas & divitiæ summa*
*rerum varietate exponuntur, Abditorum effectuum Causæ acri indagine*
*inquisitæ demonstrantur, cognitæ per Artis & Naturæ conjugium ad*
*Humanæ vitæ necessarium usum vario Experimentorum apparatu,*
*necnon novo modo & ratione applicantur.*

AD

# ALEXANDRUM VII.
## PONT. OPT. MAX.

EDITIO TERTIA,

Ad fidem scripti exemplaris recognita, & prioribus emendatior : tum ab Auctore Româ
submissis variis Observationibus novisque Figuris auctior.

## TOMUS I.

*AMSTELODAMI,*

Apud JOANNEM JANSSONIUM à WAESBERGE & FILIOS,
ANNO cIɔ Iɔc LXXVIII. *Cum Privilegiis.*

*13*

## Athanasius Kircher

Athanasius Kircher was a seventeenth-century scholar, who wrote some spectacularly illustrated and encyclopaedic accounts of the workings of nature. He wrote in Latin, which would have made his work accessible to a broad educated audience. In *Mundus Subterraneus* – the subterranean world – published in 1664 (Figure 19), Kircher imagined the interior of Planet Earth, and made links between things he had seen at the surface, such as the active volcanoes of Italy, with speculations as to the internal workings of the globe. He published the first map to show the distribution of volcanoes around the world, and used the observation of 'the prodigious Volcanos, or fire-belching mountains; the eruptions of sulphurous fires not only out of the Earth, but also out of the very Sea; the multitude of hot Baths everywhere' to reason that volcanoes could not originate 'in the Air, not in the Water, nay, nor as the Vulgar persuade themselves, not at the bottom of Mountains, but in the very in-most privy-Chambers and retiring places of the Earth', where Vulcan has his 'Elaboratories, Shops and Forges in the profoundest Bowels of Nature' (Figure 20).[18] The florid language may not have been Kircher's, as this version was published as a part of a short pamphlet on volcanoes in the aftermath of the great eruption of Mount Etna in 1669 (see Chapter 2), but it conjures up a clear picture of the interpretation.

Kircher was clearly very much influenced by progress in the field of medicine at the time (the circulation of the blood, for example), and his depictions of Earth show how a permanent source of fire and heat at the centre of the Earth might feed a series of smaller bodies of fire throughout the interior of the planet, and how where these hot fluids burst forth they might be the underlying cause of volcanoes.

Kircher was working at a time when there were no ways of gathering information about the deep workings of the planet. Today, we can use measurements of Earth's gravity and magnetic field across the surface of the planet to get a fuzzy idea of what might be happening at depth. More routinely, seismologists can study the ways in which large earthquakes send waves of energy through the body of the Earth. And in just the same way that a medical scientist might use X-rays to examine the three-dimensional structure of the human body, seismologists can now produce computed-tomography (CT) scans of the interior of the planet. Our contemporary understanding of the nature of Earth's interior is also that it is dynamic and changing, and driven to a large extent by the loss of heat from the hot core at the centre of the planet.

Kircher's descriptions of the workings of volcanoes were based on his own first-hand knowledge. In 1638, he had scrambled up to the crater of Vesuvius at night and peered into its steaming crater. It had erupted just seven years earlier, and was still in an active state: 'The crater was terrible to behold. It was lit up by the fires and the glowing sulphur and bitumen produced an intolerable vapour.'[19]

Shortly before arriving at Vesuvius, Kircher had also visited the lava-covered lower slopes of Mount Etna, the erupting volcano of Stromboli and seen the after-effects of a series of great earthquakes that struck Calabria in March to June of that year. Kircher's cut-away sketches of volcanoes were among the first depictions of volcanoes that tried to show the links between what could be seen at or above the surface and speculation as to what might be happening below. This cut-away style was still popular a century later, and used to great effect by Spallanzani (see Chapter 3) and many others.

Figure 20   Athanasius Kircher's vision of the world's volcanoes being fed by fires connected to a central source of heat inside the Earth. *Mundus subterraneus*, 1664. Oxford, Bodleian Library, Douce K 149, V.1–V.2.

**Systema Ideale PYROPHYLACIORUM** Subterraneorum, quorum montes Vulcanii, veluti spiracula quædam existant.

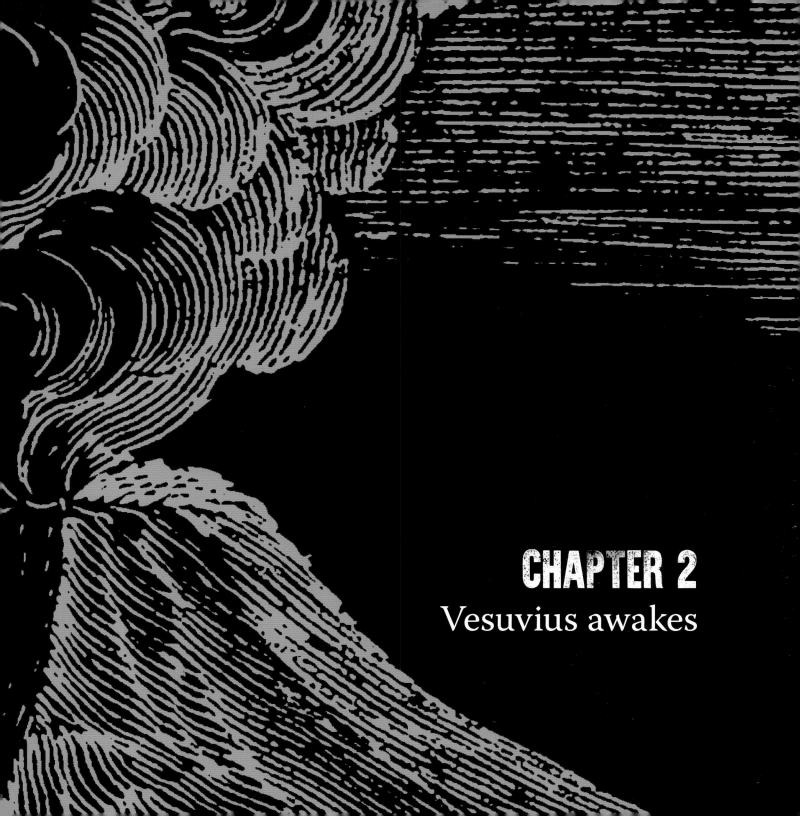

# CHAPTER 2
## Vesuvius awakes

AFTER THE DRAMATIC ERUPTION of 79 CE, Vesuvius rumbled on for many decades, but left little documentary trace. Ecclesiastical accounts appear to describe some substantial eruptions between the fifth and twelfth centuries, including a major explosive eruption in 472, and a major lava flow in 787. Many years later, towards the end of the sixteenth century the small but violent eruption on the outskirts of modern-day Naples that formed the Monte Nuovo in the Phlegrean Fields (Chapter 1) provided a brief indication of the damaging potential of their neighbouring volcanoes.

## December 1631

The eruption of 1631 began with little warning on the morning of 16 December. Vesuvius had been dormant for many years, and what was known of Vesuvius was probably derived mainly from the writings of the ancient philosophers such as Pliny the Elder and his nephew.

The eruption rapidly reached an explosive climax, depositing blocks of pumice and ash in a swathe to the north and east of the volcano. The eruption continued with intensity the next day, with hot, pyroclastic clouds descending the flanks of the volcano and reaching as far as the bay of Naples. Heavy rains accompanied the eruption, causing extensive landslides, mudflows and flooding, and leading to many thousands of casualties. At least 20,000 people are thought to have been displaced from their homes and as many as 4,000 died, mostly in the pyroclastic clouds of 17 December. Cardinals of the church took charge of managing the crisis; the blood of San Gennaro, the patron saint of Naples, was reported to have become liquefied at the time.

Figure 21   Images of Vesuvius before and after the eruption of 1631 CE, showing San Gennaro looking over the mountain. From Joannes Masculus, *De incendio Vesuvii*, 1633. Oxford, Bodleian Library, D 9.15 Linc. (prelims).

Cuncta iacent flammis, et tristi mersa fauilla.

*Statius Montis Vesuuij post vltimu Incendium.*

Hic est pampineis viridis modo Vesuius umbris.

*Status Montis Vesuuij ante vltimum Incendium.*

Mount ÆTNA or MONGIBELLO in Sicily
beeing A True Draught of yͤ Eruption in 1669.

A. Mountaines raysed by the Eruption
B. The Eruptions
C. Arch of Mount Marcello
D. The Castle of Catania
E. The Fiery Current falling into yͤ Sea

Tre Castagno
ruined
Puñta
Slueio
Via grande
V. Verde
S. Antoni
S. Agatta
Patanei
S. Grigoli
Nizeti
Tre Mistreri
Podara
ruined
S. Nicola
ruined
Mascal
Fladie
Vatate
Monpelier
Fallichi
la Nuncrata
S. Giovanni
S. Sophia
laGuardi
li Portielli
S. Antonio

A   B   A

CATANIA

This short-lived but dramatic eruption heralded the re-awakening of Vesuvius, which then continued to erupt on and off until 1944. It also sparked a huge publishing boom, with multiple pamphlets, reports and illustrations of accounts of the eruption being printed in Naples and across Europe. In this regard, the 1631 eruption may have been the first major natural disaster to have made European 'news', and many years later the event was still well known to natural historians.

By the time of the Grand Tour, Vesuvius was a well-known landmark and tourist destination. One early tourist, William Bromley, described a visit in 1688. 'After an ascent for three miles, partly on horse and for the most part up to the middle of my legs in ashes',[20] he came upon a view of the active cone,

> a mountain out of the top of which is a constant smoak. There have been 22 eruptions, and of late years they are observed to be much more frequent than formerly. When they happen they are very dreadful, not only in respect of the noise, but the consequences, having burned two or three cities or villages. They always shake the windows and doors in Naples. The mountain is always on fire, and near it are huge stones, so cinerated as to be of incredible lightness.[21]

The draw of Vesuvius and its surroundings would only have grown after the discovery of the buried cities of Herculaneum and Pompeii in the mid-eighteenth century.

Figure 22 Late-seventeenth-century print of a contemporary drawing of the great 1669 eruption of Mount Etna, showing the new cinder cones formed during the eruption and the lavas reaching Catania and flowing out to sea. © Ashmolean Museum, University of Oxford.

### Etna, 1669

On 11 March 1669, a violent and dramatic eruption began on the lower slopes of Mount Etna, near to the present-day Nicolosi (Figure 22) on the island of Sicily. Two completely new craters formed, building the substantial cinder cone of Monti Rossi, and the fountains of red-hot cinders and the great fissure that opened along the volcano flanks fed a huge flow of lava that slowly advanced towards the sea. Eventually, the lava flows reached and then engulfed a major part of the port town of Catania, crossing over its 20-metre-high walls and displacing many tens of thousands of people in its path. This eruption, which was probably the largest eruption of Etna of the past 2,000 years, was observed at close hand by Francesco D'Arezzo, a poet and playwright from Syracuse, with an interest in chemistry. He was expecting to find that the lavas were made of bitumen and sulphur, but found instead that they lacked the smell of boiling sulphur and they were 'nothing else but glass … or rocks or other stuff vitrified'.[22]

The third Earl of Winchilsea, Heneage Finch, witnessed the eruption from Catania, at the foot of Etna, on his way back to Britain from a posting as the Ambassador to Constantinople (Figure 23). He described the tremendous scale of the 'inundation of fire', extending as it did for '15 miles in length and 7 in breadth', and the ways that the lava advanced for a considerable distance into the sea 'causing a great and horrible noise, smoak and hissing'. He also describes very clearly that way that lava flows on Etna form prominent ridges or levees along their margins: 'It formed a passage like to a river, with its banks on each side very steep and craggy, and in this channel moves the greatest quantity of this fire, which is the most liquid, with stones of the same composition and cinders all red hot swimming upon the fire.'[23]

### William Hamilton

William Hamilton, a Scottish nobleman, arrived in Naples in 1764, taking up the role of His Britannic Majesty's Envoy Extraordinary to the Kingdom of the Two Sicilies. This was a post he held for thirty-seven years. Among his several residences in and around Naples was the Villa Angelica at Portici, at the foot of Vesuvius and well within reach of the ancient sites of Pompeii and Herculaneum, which were actively under excavation at that time.

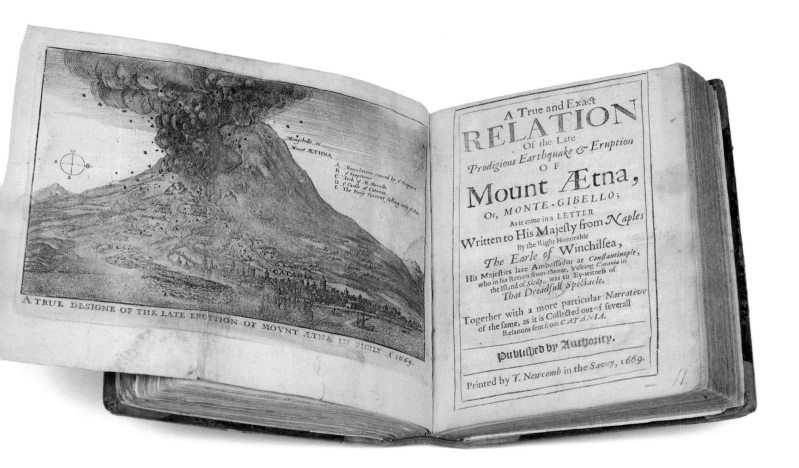

Figure 23   The eruption of Mount Etna in 1669, from *A true and exact relation of the late prodigious earthquake & eruption of Mount Aetna…* By Heneage Finch, Earl of Winchilsea, Oxford, Bodleian Library, G.Pamph. 1499 (11).

This diplomatic role was not well paid, but offered Hamilton the chance to live in a pleasant climate and to develop his interests in art, history and natural science. From the time that he arrived, in November 1764, he 'attended to the particular changes of Mount Vesuvius'. Vesuvius was, then, in a state of agitation, with frequent eruptions of both lava and 'fire fountaining' episodes. For the first year of observation, little was going on at the volcano, and Hamilton was able to ascend to the summit and peer into the 'mouth of the volcano, the sides of which were incrusted with salts and minerals of various colours white, green, deep and pale yellow'. In March 1766, 'the smoke increased and was mixed with ashes, which fell and did great damage to the vinyards' near the volcano. On 28 March 1766, 'the lava began to boil over the mouth of the volcano. It was preceded by a violent explosion, and a shower of red-hot stones and cinders were thrown up to a great height'. Hamilton stayed on the mountain the whole night, reporting that 'the lava had the appearance of a river of red-hot and liquid metal, on which were large floating cinders, half lighted and rolling one over another forming a most beautiful cascade'. A few days later he described the peculiar features of lava – that while it is certainly fluid, it also has a considerable strength – 'The lava was of such a consistency, though it appeared as liquid as water, as almost to resist the impression of a long stick; and large stones thrown on it with all my force did not sink, but making a slight impression, floated on the surface.' He also described the way the lava flowed into tubes, and that the flow front looked 'like a heap of red hot coals forming a wall'.[24] After the eruption had finished, and the products cooled, Hamilton went back to the crater where the lava had emerged and collected some of the salts that had precipitated on and around the vent.

Encouraged by the reception that his letters received (they were published in the journal of the Royal Society of London), Hamilton continued his observations and reports, and began a systematic programme of sample collection and sketching to capture the steady changes to the volcanic cone, in the main crater of Vesuvius, and of the main features of the eruptions.

In 1776, Hamilton published a wonderful illustrated volume documenting the recent eruptions of Vesuvius called *Campi Phlegraei: observations on the volcanos of the two Sicilies.* This was one of the first descriptive monographs of an active volcano, and was particularly distinguished for the vividly coloured gouache paintings by Pietro Fabris,

Figure 24 *previous page* Eruption of lava from the flanks of Vesuvius, 23 December 1760 to 8 January 1761. William Hamilton used this image to show that volcanoes many not always erupt from their summit. Hamilton, *Campi Phlegraei*, 1776. Oxford, Bodleian Library, Vet. F5 b.2, plate 12.

Figure 25 Eruption of Vesuvius on 9 August 1779, seen from Naples. Gouache by Pietro Fabris, from the supplement to the 1779 edition of William Hamilton's *Campi Phlegraei*. Oxford, Bodleian Library, Vet. F5 b.2, Tavola III.

many of which feature Hamilton dressed in a red coat and with a cane (see Figure 9). Hamilton published a supplement three years after the great eruption of Vesuvius of August 1779.

In 1805, Alexander von Humboldt (see Chapter 4) and Simón Bolívar visited Vesuvius, and Humboldt was fortunate enough to see the opening phases of a paroxysmal Strombolian eruption on 12 August.

## 1817 eruption

Vesuvius remained an essential fixture on the Grand Tour for many years, and must have made an excellent source of tourist memorabilia. Jane Waldie wrote of her ascent to the summit in 1817:

> The summit of Vesuvius is a wide circular plain, strewed all over with huge masses of lava. One of these rocks forms a sort of cavern considerable enough to contain several persons, and is the only spot which was perfectly secure from the tremendous showers of stones and cinders that were almost momentarily exploded … On arriving at the plain, the noise and rumbling became quite distinct and added greatly to the horror of the scene. Through every crevice flame or smoke issued out, and we could perceive the red-hot lava slowly running beneath the thin broken crust on which we trod, and which was so hot as to burn the shoes on our feet.[25]

She also described the custom of folding coins into the lava, to create souvenirs:

> My brother and sister drew out a small quantity of lava at the end of a long stick. Into this they stuck some copper coins, and the flexile lava enclosed them within itself and turned them to a bright green. Many persons who have seen them, have been simple enough to ask whether these coins were thrown out of the mountain also, concluding the King of Naples had established a mint in Vesuvius.[26]

Figure 26   Sketch of street dwellers ('lazzaroni') in Naples 'on a Sunday', 1821. Watercolour by John Gardner Wilkinson, who later became a prominent Egyptologist. Oxford, Bodleian Library, MS. Wilkinson dep. d. 8, fol. 2r. © National Trust.

azaroni, Naples, on a Sunday.
September –

## 1834 eruption

Charles Daubeny, a professor of chemistry and botany at the University of Oxford, visited Vesuvius late in 1834, after a particularly large eruption of lava. This had erupted from a vent near that of the 1817 eruption, and had eventually buried 180 houses and 500 acres of land. Daubeny built a field apparatus to collect some of the gases from the now long-cooling lava flow, and reported finding large quantities of hydrochloric acid, ammonium chloride and carbon dioxide, and smaller amounts of copper chloride and iron oxides – just the same species that one can find being emitted from cooling lava flows on Mount Etna today, for example. He also excavated through the blocky cover of the lava flow, and measured the temperature of the warm lava body using a pyrometer, a device for measuring very high temperatures, which had been modified from a design used in china clay furnaces.

As a chemist, Daubeny had previously been strongly influenced by the ideas of Humphrey Davy (inventor of the Davy safety lamp), and his chemical theory of volcanic action which posited that volcanic eruptions were caused by the heat generated during the reaction of metals with water (see Chapter 4). Daubeny's new observations shed no new light on this chemical theory; but his new conclusion, that 'atmospheric air and water both find their way to the seat of volcanic operations' is one that remains current today.[27]

## 1906 eruption

The last major eruption of Vesuvius, before it eventually returned to a dormant state in 1944, was the eruption of 1906. This was a very significant eruption, which caught the attention of Frank Perret, an American engineer and inventor who had travelled to Italy in late 1903 due to his poor health. He lived at Torre del Greco, near the foot of Vesuvius, and the good view of the main cone caught his imagination. He first climbed to the summit in January 1904, and began documenting and photographing the activity. His interest in the volcano led to him being appointed Honorary Assistant to the Royal Observatory, in a role where he helped the observatory director to record the ever-evolving activity of the volcano.

As the activity ramped up towards a major paroxysmal phase of eruption, Perret described a spectrum of new phenomena for the first time – from smoke rings to

Figure 27  Tourists on Vesuvius being carried up in improvised sedan chairs. Frank Perret, *Vesuvio*, 1906. Oxford, Bodleian Library, EV 55(L) (Buxton Room), plate 7.

Figure 28 *An Eruption of Vesuvius*, 1774, by Joseph Wright of Derby. University College of Wales, Aberystwyth, Wales / Bridgeman Images.

'flashing arcs', caused by shock waves in the erupting ash plume, and St Elmo's fire, as strongly electrified ash clouds clipped past the observatory.

A few days before the eruption began, Perret noted how at night in bed he thought he could hear a continuous buzzing sound which seemed to come from below. By placing his teeth against the iron bedstead, he confirmed his hunch – this was almost certainly the detection of volcanic 'tremor', a continuous seismic hum that moving magma creates inside volcanoes shortly before eruption begins. During the eruption itself Perret and a few other observatory staff lived on-site in the Royal Vesuvian Observatory, which he found 'a period of trying, tedious, comparatively unexciting living with intense discomfort and suffering'.[28]

This was just the beginning of Perret's forty-year career as an experimental volcanologist, which took him around the world, and stimulated the invention of a host of new techniques for collecting samples from erupting volcanoes and measuring their activity.

## Vesuvius and popular culture

Among the many travellers attracted to the volcanic spectacle of Vesuvius in eruption were some of the great landscape artists of the eighteenth and nineteenth centuries including Joseph Wright of Derby. Wright stayed with Hamilton for four weeks in October 1774, a period of time characterized by the slow but continuous eruption of lava flows. Wright was impressed, writing to his brother that 'there was a very considerable eruption at the time – tis the most wonderful sight in nature'.[29] His 1774 painting, *An Eruption of Vesuvius* (Figure 28), captures very clearly the vivid jets of incandescent material uplighting the steam and gas plumes from the summit of the Grand Cone, and the dull red cascade of blocky lava descending the flanks of the cone and crossing the plain of Vesuvius's crater. But the style and scale of this eruption was insignificant compared with the dramatic outbursts of 1765 and 1779 captured by Pietro Fabris and William Hamilton.

For those not fortunate enough to travel, there were many other ways to enjoy the spectacle of volcanoes in the 1700s, with plays, music and great public displays of 'firework' volcanoes. One master firework-maker was the Italian Giovanni Battista

Torré. From 1772 to 1774, he was the resident pyrotechnician in the Marylebone pleasure gardens of central London. His masterpiece was called the 'Forge of Vulcan' and, by all accounts, was a vivid firework display built around a representation of the blazing magmatic hearth of Mount Etna, Sicily. James Boswell recounts a visit by the diarist Samuel Johnson: 'His curiosity having been excited by the praises bestowed on the celebrated Torré's fireworks at Marylebone gardens, he desired Mr Stevens to accompany him thither.' Unfortunately, Johnson was left disappointed, as 'the evening had proved showery and the [exhibits] were so thoroughly water soaked that it was impossible any part of the exhibition should be made'.[30]

## The first volcanic photograph

In the digital era of instant communication, breaking news of volcanic eruptions usually arrives image-first. Every year, new volcanic eruptions in far-flung places make the prime-time news, simply because of the glorious multicolour spectacle. But the arrival of photography, and more particularly of cameras that could capture action shots sufficiently quickly, is still relatively recent. And, just as in the case of William Hamilton, Vesuvius was perhaps the first volcano where an explosive volcanic eruption was caught on print (Figure 29).

The April 1872 eruption of Vesuvius, Italy, was one of the most violent paroxysms at Vesuvius during the nineteenth century. The eruption was quickly documented by Luigi Palmieri, who was director of the Vesuvius Observatory from 1852 to 1896. His report of the eruption contains a dramatic line drawing of Vesuvius in eruption on 26 April, with a caption that suggests that it was based on a photograph taken in Naples.

Some years later, John Wesley Judd, who was a volcanologist and professor of geology at the Royal School of Mines, published an influential textbook on volcanoes. In this, he included a woodcut of the April 1872 eruption of Vesuvius, which had been engraved directly from a photograph, and commented that 'on the occasion of this outburst, the aid of instantaneous photography was first made available for obtaining a permanent record of the appearances displayed at volcanic eruptions'.[31] This immediately opened up the opportunity for observers to capture the detail of what was happening in a way that might be considered less prone to exaggeration, and also to capture the ways that phenomena might change from instant to instant, or through time. A photograph from the same sequence later became a 'stock' volcano photograph, appearing in many volcano textbooks of the late nineteenth and early twentieth centuries. The original photographer is likely to have been Giorgio Sommer, who ran a studio in Naples.

Like all new technologies, it took a little while for cameras to become sufficiently portable to be widely used to document volcanic eruptions. One early adopter and volcano enthusiast was the splendidly named Tempest Anderson, an ophthalmologist and inveterate travel-photographer in the late nineteenth century. Anderson's scientific volcano photography included the documenting of the aftermath of the devastating eruptions of Soufrière, St Vincent, in 1902 (see Figures 67–69) and Vesuvius in 1906, and his extensive archive of glass photographic plates includes a copy of that first photograph of the 1872 eruption (Figure 29). In 1913, Tempest Anderson died on board a ship in the Red Sea on his way back from a tour of south-east Asia, which had taken him round many of the volcanoes of Java and the Philippines. He found many of the volcanoes a little disappointing as the cones were deeply weathered and covered with impassable jungle. One exception to this was Krakatau, which had erupted just thirty years before and was still almost bare of vegetation, so that the precipitous cliff face created during the eruption 'shows every vein, dyke, and intrusive sheet like a diagram'.[32]

Figure 29   Glass slide of *Vesuvius in Eruption* in April 1872, from Tempest Anderson's collection. © York Museums Trust.

Vesuvius, in
eruption

A: 1637.

# CHAPTER 3
## The origins of lava

I N 1565, CONRAD GESSNER, a Swiss naturalist, published the first known sketches of a curious form of 'prismatic basalt', that was a 'basalt stone, consisting of at least four and most seven corners' (Figure 30).[33] The sketch was of some rocks that had been discovered in Saxony by Johannes Kentmann, a sixteenth-century German physician and natural historian. Gessner's sketch has captured the general shapes of these columns, although they tend not to have pointed tips, and poses the obvious question: how do such regular prismatic basalts form? They have such regular forms; are they not fossil organisms, or giant crystals? And if they are so regular, how they can bear any relation to the swirling flows of lava that cascade down the sides of volcanoes? Answering these questions proved to be remarkably difficult, and took many decades of careful detective work by natural historians and early geologists across Europe.

## Polygonal rocks

Volcanic rocks come in all shapes and sizes. On the slopes of a young volcano it is easy to trace the solidified trails left by long-frozen lava flows, if the vegetation allows. And, once you know what you are looking for, it can be a simple task to spot the layers of volcanic pumice in road cuttings along the volcano flanks. The way that volcanologists tend to work in the field is that they can recognize the patterns made by particular sorts of volcanic deposit and then link those to the events that have produced similar deposits during observed volcanic eruptions.

But how do we go about understanding the nature of volcanic rocks that perhaps were not ever erupted, or erupted in ways that no one has seen before? One of the most striking and puzzling volcanic rock types are those that form spectacular jointed

Figure 30 'Prismatic basalt' and an example of polygonal columnar joints in lava from Germany. Conrad Gessner, *De Rerum Fossilium*, 1565. Oxford, Bodleian Library, RR. z. 25, fols. 20v–21r.

*salten repræsentant: cuius hanc figuram Io-*
*annes Kentmanus mihi communicauit. E*
*subiectis verò duobus paruis, minor Adamā-*
*tis Cyprij nomine ex Italia ad me missus est.*
*est autem vilis lapillus, aut fluor potius, Ad-*
*amanti vel Crystallo persimilis, albus, pelluci-*
*dus, purus. Maioris mẽtio fiet infrà mox post*
*finitam de Basalte tractationem.*

Plinius lib. 36. cap. 7. inter marmo-
ra: Inuenit (inquit) Aegyptus in Aethiopia quem vocant Basalten, ferrei
coloris atꝗ duritiæ. vñde & nomé ei
dedit. Nunquam hic maior repertus
est, quàm in templo Pacis, ab impera-
tore Vespasiano Augusto dicatus: argumento Nili xvj. liberis circà luden-
tibus, per quos totidem cubiti sum-
mi incremẽti augentis se amnis eius
intelliguntur. Non absimilis illi nar-
raꞇ in Thebis delubro Serapis, vt pu-
tant Memnonis statua dicatus: quem
quotidiano Solis ortu contactũ Solis radijs crepare dicunt.      Hæc illa.
Quinꝗ

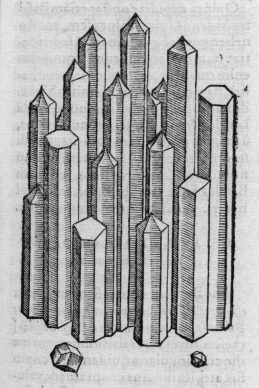

'columns', or colonnades, like those of the Giant's Causeway, in Antrim, Northern Ireland. When looked at from above, these columns form a great tessellated platform of interlocking polygons – mostly four-, five- or six-sided shapes (see Figure 33). The rock type here is a basalt: a hot magma that would have squeezed into place, a little bit below ground, about 60 million years ago. Although the remarkable regularity of the pattern might make it look as though it is man-made, in fact rocks showing these same sorts of patterns can be found all around the world.

In a description of the Giant's Causeway in 1694, the Reverend Dr Samuel Foley, bishop of Down and Connor in Antrim, writes: 'It consists of many thousands of pillars, almost all pentagonal or hexagonal. The pillars are some 15, some 18 inches, some 2 foot in diameter, every pillar consists of several joynts or pieces. The tops of them looks very like the pavements that are in some gentlemens halls.'[34] He declared it a fossil or mineral of stone and not of the animal or vegetable kingdoms.

Thomas Molyneux, an Irish naturalist and physician, spotted that the stones of the Giant's Causeway were very similar in 'colour, hardness and substance' to those described by Pliny from 'Aethiopia' and by Kentmann from Germany, and agreed that they most closely resemble basalts. 'This stone is of an extraordinary hard, close and compact texture: its grain so very even and fine … it seems as if it were one plain homogeneous body. It has in perfection that quality of the Lapidus Basanus or Touchstone … for showing the various impressions different metals make upon it when rubbed or drawn along its surface.'[35]

Having established that these were rocks, rather than fossils or minerals, still left the question of how they were formed.

These prismatic, or polygonally jointed, rocks attracted much attention in the mid- to late eighteenth century, when the question of their nature and origins was once again under scrutiny. At this time there were different schools of thought about both the order in which rocks had formed and the processes by which they had been formed. In the 'Neptunist' school, promoted by Abraham Werner, the idea was that the rocks of the Earth had formed progressively from an ocean that had once covered the whole Earth. In this theory, the oldest rocks were the crystalline rocks that had precipitated first from the ocean, while younger volcanic rocks had been formed locally, by the burning of coal beds. In this theory, crystalline basalts and volcanic rocks had quite different origins. In

Figure 31 Cut-away image of the crater on the island of Vulcano, the Aeolian Islands, Italy, showing the pentagonal prismatic columns. From Lazzaro Spallanzani's *Viaggi alle Due Sicilie*, 1793. Oxford, Bodleian Library, Vet. F5 e.9 (t.2), plate 5.

TAB. V.

*Vulcano.*

Ios. Lanfranchi R. I. Univ̇er. Pap. Pict. del.

Anderloni S.

Figure 32   Sketch of the extinct volcano of the Coupe de Jaujac in the Ardeche, showing a lava flow feeding a pavement of prismatic basalts. Faujas de St Fond, *Recherches sur les volcans éteints du Vivarais et du Velay*, 1778. Oxford, Bodleian Library, 18823 b.1.

contrast, the 'Plutonist' school suggested that crystalline rocks were formed by deep-seated magmatic or 'plutonic' activity. In this theory, basalts could be either volcanic, if erupted, or plutonic, if intruded. A resolution of the origins of basalts, and of the links between glassy and crystalline basalts, came about after studies of the young volcanic rocks of France and Germany.

In 1751, the French Natural Historian Jean-Étienne Guettard travelled through the Auvergne region of France. He noticed some unusually porous and dark rocks, which he identified as lavas, and presented a paper the next year to the French Royal Academy of Sciences on the topic of 'some volcanic mountains in France'. The discovery that the hills of the Auvergne were volcanic made this region a magnet for the field study of ancient volcanoes, and attracted much attention in the later eighteenth and early nineteenth centuries. Observations in the Auvergne provided the critical evidence in resolving the links between the many different forms of basalt that can be found in volcanoes.

Volcanic rocks were being discovered in Germany, too. Rudolph Raspe had a great interest in geology as a student, and by the late 1760s was a professor and librarian in Kassel and curator of antiquities for Frederick II of Hesse-Kassel. In 1771, Raspe published observations on some basalt rocks near Kassel, Germany: 'I have discovered several hills composed of basalt rocks, formed in polyhedrous and mostly pentagonal columns. Our rocks differ from those of the Giants Causeway, for their want of articulation, and from those in Egypt described by Strabo.' Raspe described how they contained nests of small crystals, but no traces of any sorts of organic remains (or fossils) and, in accordance with prevailing ideas at the time, suggested that he had first thought that they might have formed by 'watery crystallisation' either 'at the first settling of the chaos, or at the time of a dissolution of the globe'.[36]

The French natural historian Nicolas Desmarest had recently described similar rocks from the Auvergne (Figure 32) and used the close association of these polygonal basalts with erupted rocks – lava and scoria – to suggest that these forms had developed during freezing of molten rock. Raspe noted that the rocks he had examined shared some similar features. The top of the hill of Wilhelmshöhe, an Italianate water park, was mainly made of 'enormous pieces of lava and scoria'. Lower down 'are found the basaltes. Many of these are formed in polyhedrous pillars'. Finding this evidence convincing, and with knowledge of similar examples at the Italian volcanoes of Bolsena and Etna, Raspe conceded that

Figure 33 Spectacular cross-sections of basalt columns at the Giant's Causeway. © Shutterstock / Gigi Peis.

he was in agreement with Desmarest's interpretation, and that the rocks in Germany, together with others from France, Sicily and Italy, could all be 'basalts from volcanoes'.[37]

Soon after, Raspe fled Germany to escape his debts, attempted unsuccessfully to join James Cook's third and final expedition to the Pacific and was eventually expelled from the Royal Society for 'divers frauds and infamy of character' when his past misdemeanours caught up with him. Raspe moved to Cornwall and later wrote the tales of Baron Munchausen, although his authorship of these fables wasn't revealed until many years after his death.

In summer 1772, Joseph Banks undertook an excursion to Iceland and on the way visited Fingal's Cave (named for the mythical Fionn mac Cumhaill) on the Scottish island of Staffa. Banks was a naturalist who had accompanied James Cook on his first voyage to the Southern Seas from 1768 to 1771. Banks was planning another South Seas adventure in 1772, but this fell through and he instead took an expedition to Iceland, via the Western Isles and Orkney. At Staffa, Banks and his companions were overcome with the spectacle, which they compared favourably to the Giant's Causeway (Figure 33): 'The mind can hardly form an idea more magnificent than such a space, supported on each side by ranges of columns; and roofed by the bottoms of those which have been broke off to form it.'[38] Banks took careful measurements of the columns, and was quite sure that this was another example of 'a coarse kind of basaltes'. Banks's travelling companion was a young man from Sweden, Uno von Troil, who later became archbishop of Uppsala. Von Troil found abundant evidence for the role 'eruptions of fire' had played in the formation of these rocks,[39] and pointed out that in many places where these basalt colonnades were found, they were associated with lavas and with fragmental volcanic rocks, or tuffs (also called tuffa).

William Hamilton made an important contribution to the discussion when he published an account of some 'volcanoes on the banks of the Rhine' which he saw during a five-day sailing trip from Bonn to Mainz in 1777. In the city of Koblenz he recognized that many of the building and paving stones used were basalt columns, often pentagonal in cross section. He also noticed that 'the walls of most of the ancient buildings in the town of Cologne were of a tuff exactly resembling that of Naples and environs'. Likewise, in Bonn: 'The stone in general use for building here is a very compact one, a hard volcanic tuffa like that … of the fort called Piperno in Italy; it is something like freestone but … is mixed with fragments of lava and other volcanic substances.'

Hamilton found evidence for each of these volcanic rock types in situ during his boat trip, and remarked that one reason that columnar-jointed lavas might not be common around Vesuvius and Naples might simply be that they had been entirely used up building the great Roman roads. 'The Appian way is mostly composed of lava of a pentagonal and hexagonal form … evidently made of pieces of such basaltic columns.' At the conclusion of his travels, Hamilton was left 'not in the least doubt but that all basaltes, wheresoever they exist, have originated from subterranean fire and are true lavas.'[40]

Figure 34  Specimens of fresh and altered volcanic ejecta found on Mount Vesuvius, and a snuff box from William Hamilton's *Campi Phlegraei*, 1776. Wellcome Library, London.

## Melting rocks

Another big step forward in trying to understand the nature of basalt came in the late 1700s, when enterprising investigators began to try to experiment on natural materials. One puzzle that needed to be solved was whether or not there was any relationship between the sort of red-hot flowing 'basalt' lavas, such as those that were pouring down the side of Vesuvius in the eighteenth century, and the dull grey crystalline basalts that can be found across many parts of the world, including in places that no longer have volcanoes. Although the field evidence was beginning to stack up, there was still no satisfactory explanation for why basalt might take so many different forms. Adding to the difficulties of answering this question were two other factors: geologists hadn't yet solved the question of geological time (not only whether time might be 'deep', but also whether all rocks had formed in a particular order, or not); and there was still no agreement on whether crystalline rocks had a watery 'Neptunian', or hot 'Plutonic' origin.

Lazzaro Spallanzani was an Italian priest and a physiologist, and by 1768 had been appointed to the Chair of Natural History at the University of Pavia. He is famous for his investigations on the nature and origin of life. He developed carefully designed experiments to test whether life could emerge spontaneously from inert matter, and carried out some practical experiments on reproduction in frogs.

In 1788, Spallanzani toured the many volcanoes of southern Italy, including Vesuvius, Etna, Stromboli and Vulcano. His primary aim was to collect some volcanic specimens for the museum at the University of Pavia, but on the way he made many careful observations of the behaviour of the volcanoes, collected samples for laboratory investigations of rock melting and freezing and made some of the first measurements of the chemical compositions of volcanic gases and lavas.

The cut-away sketches of the volcanoes that he visited on his travels, and which he published in a series of books, are wonderfully observed. They are similar in style to the cut-away images by Athanasius Kircher (Figure 35), and there is a clear attempt in Spallanzani's sketches to represent the sorts of things that might be happening deep within the volcanoes (Figure 36).

Spallanzani developed many interesting ideas about volcanoes, and was both one of the earliest chemical analysts of volcanic materials and one of the first experimentalists

Figure 35  Cut-away image of Mount Etna, 1637. Athanasius Kircher, *Mundus Subterraneus*, 1678. Oxford, Bodleian Library, Douce K 149, opp. p. 200.

PUS MONTIS
ÆTNÆ
b Authore
Observati
A.º 1637.

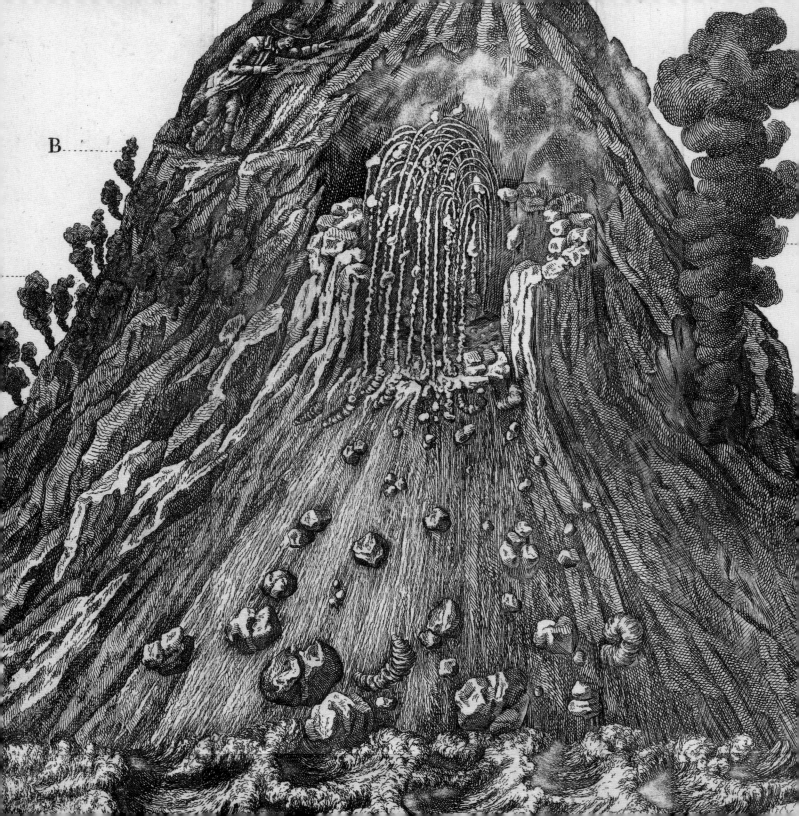

on volcanic rocks. He tried heating various different sorts of volcanic and other rocks in a glass furnace. He left samples in the furnace for up to three months, and observed how some samples would change when heated. Some materials slowly turned to a glass; others melted and boiled, but retained a consistency so firm that they couldn't be poured out of the crucible, nor could he make an impression on them with a metal wire. When the glass furnace didn't have much effect on some of the lavas, he ran experiments in a much more powerful fire: a chemical reverberatory furnace, used for smelting metals at very high temperatures. In this furnace, samples of lava became soft and fluid, and could be poured out of the crucible; to Spallanzani this was a proof of the intensity of the heat required to drive a volcano.

Satisfied that he could now understand the link between heat and the rocky products of volcanoes, Spallanzani extended his investigations and experiments to look at the gases associated with volcanoes. He extracted a 'small quantity of limpid liquor' from some glassy spotted obsidian lavas from Lipari. He tested a drop of the liquid on his tongue and decided that it tasted like dilute hydrochloric acid. He then ran a series of diagnostic chemical tests to prove this. Surprised 'at the presence of this salt and this water within a stony substance', he repeated the experiment with a larger quantity of the same rock, but powdered, and also with a different form of Lipari obsidian. Both samples also released hydrochloric acid and water. The lavas from Vesuvius, Etna and Stromboli that he tested also contained traces of hydrochloric acid, while a manufactured glass did not, leading to the clear conclusion that 'this acid originates ... perhaps from the sea penetrating beneath the volcanic mountains'.[41] Spallanzani's observations and conclusions are extraordinary for their insight: magmas do indeed contain quantities of dissolved chemical species that are gaseous at the high temperatures at which magma erupts, and that condense as liquids at lower temperatures. And magmas from subduction zones, in settings such as the Pacific Ring of Fire and the Aeolian Islands of Italy, do indeed tend to be enriched in both water and chlorine, which ultimately will have come from seawater.

Figure 36  Cut-away image of Stromboli, showing steaming and smoking vents on the sides of the volcano, the erupting central crater and the 'Sciara del Fuoco' scar that runs down the north face of the island. Lazzaro Spallanzani, *Viaggi alle Due Sicilie*, 1793. Oxford, Bodleian Library, Vet. F5 e.9 (t.2), plate 3.

## Field examples

Today, we are familiar with the many different ways in which magmas of a single composition may erupt, and the very different physical forms of the material once it is frozen. Basalt is magma that is poor in silica (silicon dioxide) but rich in iron and magnesium. It is invariably dark coloured (grey to black) when cold, and will freeze to a glass, but only if it is quenched in water. Tops of lava flows will be made up of bubbly clinker and rubble, since gas bubbles are able to expand more freely when there is less weight of rock confining them. The deep interiors of lava flows are much more likely to be dense and finely crystalline, since any gas bubbles may have time to rise and escape before the material freezes, and in the slowly cooled middle of the flow there is ample time for tiny crystals to form and grow. It is usually only the interiors of lava flows that will form the colonnades of polyhedrally jointed igneous rock as the magma cools and shrinks. And, as we have seen from the debates of the eighteenth century, it is essential to understand the spatial relationships of the different forms of basalt, in order to work out how they formed. Rocks that are rich in silica, such as rhyolite, can also erupt in a variety of different textural forms. At one end of the spectrum, the perfect glassy form of rhyolite is called obsidian, and will be well known to *Minecraft* fans. Obsidian can be perfectly deep black in colour, but can also be silky grey if it contains tiny elongated bubbles. Other forms of obsidian can also contain spectacular white spheres, or radiating 'snow flakes', made of minerals such as feldspar and quartz. More usually, rhyolite may erupt as grey lavas or bubbly pumice, which can range in colour from brilliant white to green, depending on its exact chemical composition. Volcanic ash, which is usually just pulverized or fragmented pumice, lava, crystals or glass, can form in eruptions of any composition, and is most usually black, grey, yellow or white when fresh.

Prismatic or polygonal columns have been found in rocks of many different compositions and styles of emplacement (Figure 37). They are common in lava flows that have erupted above ground. They can also be found in some great ignimbrite outflow sheets, which would have been erupted explosively as a dense violent current of ash and pumice, and then deposited while it was still hot enough for the tiny fragments of glass and ash to stick together and become firmly welded into a rigid rock.

Figure 37   Blister of young polygonally jointed lavas from Afar, Ethiopia, disturbed by faulting in 2005. © David M. Pyle.

Molten magma will always contract a little as it cools. In a magma that is crystalline, or rigid, the contraction sets up stresses that can only be relieved by fracturing the rock. These fractures will usually form perpendicular to the surface that is losing heat to the surroundings, and will then grow into the magma body below as that, too, becomes rigid. Under the right sets of conditions, the process of cooling and solidifying magma will spontaneously form columns at right angles to the cooling surface. The numbers of faces that the columns will have, and the size of the columns, will depend on the rate of cooling.

In a stationary lava flow, columns should form perpendicular to the top surface of the flow. This is, indeed, what we find in some places on Earth today, where sheets of basalt lava have flooded out across a surface. There are some great examples in the Afar region of Ethiopia, where young basalt lavas have erupted out of long fissures and fractures, flowed across the ground and air-cooled. Columnar joints pervade the upper surfaces of these young lava flows and form immediately below the glassy crust on the top surfaces of the lava flow (Figure 37).

In the Cabo de Gata of southern Spain, you can see a wonderful sliver of volcanoes wrenched out of the sea since they formed underwater about 10 million years ago. Here, there are many fabulous colonnades of polygonally jointed lavas, many of which would originally have erupted either underwater or within the wet sands of the sea floor at the time. Here, the spectacular fans of columnar joints trace out the dome shape of the original lava bodies. At Playa Monsul, the location in *Indiana Jones and the Last Crusade* where Sean Connery fends off an aerial attack with the help of an umbrella and a flock of seagulls, polygonally jointed dykes criss-cross a fabulous series of yellow and black submarine lavas.

More examples of prismatic joints can be found at high latitudes and high elevations, where lava has poured out of the volcano and come into contact with snow and ice. Here, distinctly jagged or hackly fractures can develop on the outer edges of lava flows, offering a firm clue as to the agents involved in the rapid freezing of the lava. In ancient rocks these features can help us work out where these rocks were erupted – whether underground, underwater or under ice and snow. Next time you are peering into the steamy crater of a volcano such as Etna (Figure 38), take a look for these tell-tale polygonal pillars.

Figure 38 The crater of Mount Etna. From Count de Bylandt Pastercamp's *Théorie de volcans*, 1836. © Ashmolean Museum, University of Oxford.

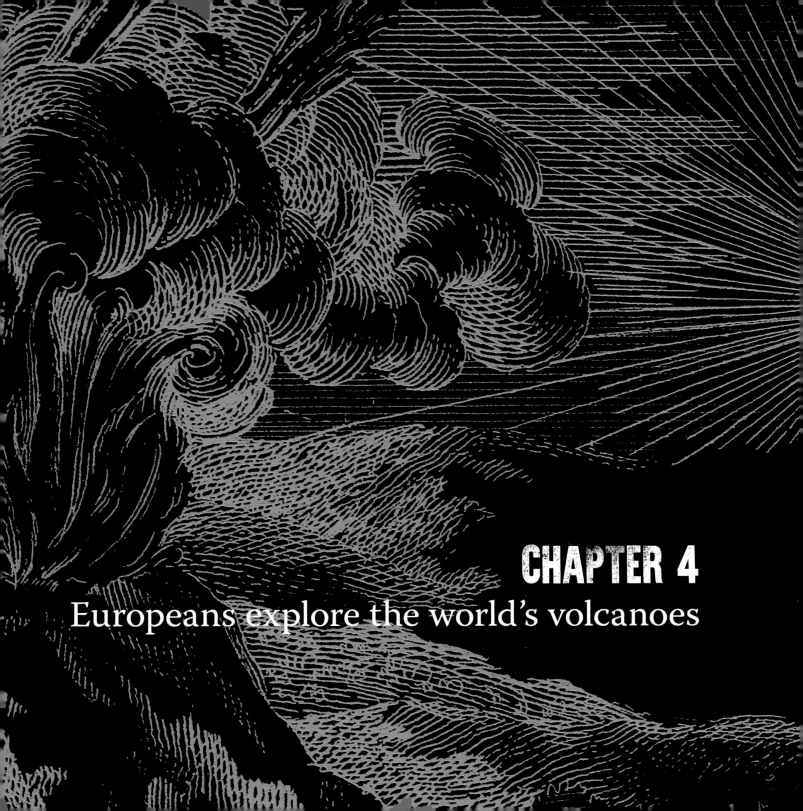

# CHAPTER 4
Europeans explore the world's volcanoes

As Europe's tentacles spread across the world, so European knowledge of the world's volcanoes grew. Modern catalogues of the dates and locations of volcanic eruptions tick off the arrival of European mariners at island volcanoes around the world, and provide the first 'historical observations' of recorded activity: Tenerife in 1492; Fogo and the Cape Verde islands in 1500; São Miguel and Pico in the Azores in 1562 and 1563. Sailors on the spice routes to the Moluccas and the easternmost volcanic islands of present-day Indonesia brought back reports of eruptions at Gamalama (or Ternate) in 1510 and Gunung Api Wetar, the 'mountain of fire', in 1512. In the sixteenth century, with the development of maps and charts for navigating the seas and of printed books, atlases and encyclopaedia of the world – such as Abraham Ortelius's atlas, *Theatrum Orbis Terrarum* (Figure 39), and Sebastian Münster's *Cosmographiae* – it became easier for the information to be stored and shared.

Many of the islands that became staging posts or stopping off points on the long journeys through the Atlantic to distant parts owe their origins to volcanic activity. Eruptions over hundreds of thousands or millions of years have slowly built up submarine mountains from the sea floor, until one day they emerge to form an island. The clusters of islands that form the Azores and the Canary Islands are all volcanic. In the Azores, new flaming islands appeared out of the sea and then disappeared again (see Chapter 5). In the Canaries, the great volcanic peak of Tenerife was a beacon for navigators, being visible from many miles away.

In the South Atlantic, neither of the volcanic islands of Ascension nor St Helena is thought to have erupted since they were first discovered in the early 1500s. St Helena has ample sources of water, and proved rather easier to inhabit and became the more usual stopping off point for ships from the East India Company on their way around the Cape of Good Hope. In contrast, Ascension is a barren island with no water and whose only food sources were fish, sea birds and turtles. A third South Atlantic volcanic island is Tristan da Cunha, discovered, like Ascension and St Helena, by the Portuguese in the early 1500s, but named after the discoverer rather than a date in the church calendar. Tristan is the most remote inhabited island in the world, and has been permanently settled since 1810. In October 1961, the eruption of a lava dome on the narrow strip of land that is the only inhabited part of the island led to the temporary evacuation of the islanders to the United Kingdom.

In the sixteenth century, Spanish colonialists travelled expansively across the New World lands of present-day Latin America, discovering for themselves what must have seemed a strange world of mountains that threw out stones, fire and brimstone. Early discoveries included the great smoking mountain of Popocatépetl in Mexico (Figure 40), climbed in the 1520s by Diego de Ordaz, who, as a reward, was allowed by Charles V to bear a smoking mountain on his coat of arms.

A little further north, a glowing lava pit in Nicaragua attracted some adventurous entrepreneurs in search of riches. Masaya is an easily accessible volcano in Nicaragua, with several very wide and deep craters at its summit. Intermittently, the craters may become filled with a roiling lava lake, and this appears to have been the case in the sixteenth century. The fiery glow of the volcano could be seen from a great distance at night, illuminating the considerable fumes from the volcano, and many stories circulated about how the red glowing material in the crater was actually molten silver or gold. In 1538, Fray Blas de Castillo was lowered into a side crater in a basket, carrying a hammer, a wooden cross and a flagon of wine. After collecting some samples from the crater floor, and discovering that the glowing vent in the centre of the crater was deeper than expected, he was pulled back out of the crater and made plans for a larger-scale metal-mining expedition. Eventually, when the governor got wind of the plan, he insisted on coming along too, and presumably there was much disappointment as the red-hot 'metal' that they managed to collect around their iron bucket turned to crumbly black 'scoria' when it cooled. Nonetheless, myths about metals continued to attract prospectors until the lava lake disappeared sometime in the 1570s. The lava lake returned in 2016, attracting flocks of visitors anew.

Figure 39 Ortelius's map of Iceland from 1585 showing Hekla in eruption. Oxford, Bodleian Library, Douce O subt. 15.

El Adelantado Don Diego de Almagro Capitan Liberali.mo

El Mar.s Don Francisco Piçarro de Truxillo

fran.co Piçarro y sus compa.s estan en la ysla Gorgona

fran.co Piçarro Sale de Panama a descubrir

fran.co Piçarro de la Puña pasa A Tumbez

Los Castellanos llegan Ala baya de San Mateo.

Los de Tumbez debaxo de Seguro dan en los Castellanos

Los Castellanos pasan a la ysla Puña

Edificase el primer templo en S.t Miguel de Piura y Her.do de Soto pelea con los ynaios

Los Castellanos pelea con los yndios en la puña

El Adelantado Don Pedro de Aluarado Badaloc

La batalla de Vtlatlan q.e dio don Pedro de Aluarado a los yndios.

Diego de Ordas Reconoce el bolcan de Tlascala

El Capitan Diego de Ordas del Reyno de Leon

# HISTORIA GENERAL DE LOS HECHOS DE LOS CASTELLANOS EN LAS ISLAS I TIERRA FIRME DEL MAR OCEANO ESCRITA POR ANTONIO D HERRERA CORONISTA MAIOR DE SV M.d D LAS INDIAS Y SV CORONISTA D. CASTILLA

## DE CADA QVARTA

## Pirates and burning islands

William Dampier was a seventeenth-century pirate who later turned his hand to exploration and writing. In 1699, he set sail in HMS *Roebuck* to try to find Terra Australis, a mythical 'southern continent'. His journey took him past the Cape of Good Hope to the north-western coast of New Holland (now Australia) and then on to Timor, New Guinea and New Britain. On the way back, he only got as far as Ascension Island before his ship sprung a leak and had to be abandoned. His crew were rescued some weeks later by a party of British naval ships on their way to Barbados. Back in England, Dampier was court-martialled for the loss of the ship, and forfeited his pay for the voyage.

Dampier wrote of his many adventures in a series of wonderfully illustrated books, the last volume of which was adorned with sketches of exotic flora and fauna and maps and charts of his route (Figure 41). The loss of the ship, and the damage to his reputation, clearly caused him concern, as he introduced his book with the words:

> The world is apt to judge of everything by the success, and whoever had ill fortune will hardly be allowed a good name. This was my unhappiness in my late expedition in the Roebuck, which foundered thro' perfect age near the island of Ascension. I suffered extreamly in my reputation by that misfortune.[42]

Despite his failure to reach the nonexistent Terra Australis, the expedition was a great success as a 'voyage of discovery', and has some lovely descriptions of burning islands – active volcanoes – that he encountered to the east of Timor island, part of what we now call the Banda Arc, and of others along the north coast of (Papua) New Guinea, part of what is now known as the Bismarck Arc. Several of his reports of the volcanoes that he encountered are the earliest surviving written records of activity at these volcanoes.

On 13 December 1699, the *Roebuck* sailed from Babao, east past Timor towards New Guinea. On 27 December Dampier recorded that:

> [they] saw the burning island … It is high but small. It runs from the sea a little sloaping towards the top, which is divided in the middle

Figure 40 Title page of the chronicles of the Spanish conquistadores showing, in the bottom right panel, Diego de Ordaz climbing Popocatépetl volcano, Mexico, in 1525. Herrera Y Tordesillas, *Historia general*, 1601. Oxford, Bodleian Library, EE 1–4 Art. III and IV.

into two peaks, between which issued out much smoak: I have not seen more from any volcano. I saw no trees; but the North side appeared green, and the rest looked barren.[43]

This is most likely Wurlali volcano, on Damar Island, Indonesia. It last erupted in 1892.

Later they sailed past another burning island, most likely Banda Api, and then around the northern coast of present-day Papua New Guinea, where they encountered for the first time several volcanoes of the New Guinea arc. On 24–25 March 1700, Dampier spent some time watching an eruption of a volcano in the straits between Papua New Guinea and New Britain:

At ten o clock I saw a great fire, blazing up in a pillar, sometimes very high for three or four minutes … In the morning I found out that the fire we had seen was a burning island, and steered for it.[44]

…

March 25th the Island all night vomited fire and smoak very amazingly and at every belch we heard a dreadful noise like thunder and saw a flame after it. The intervals between its belches were about half a minute. Some more, some less, neither were these pulses of eruptions alike, for some were but faint convulsions in comparison of the more vigorous yet even the weakest vented a great deal of fire, but the largest made a roaring noise and sent up a large flame 20 or 30 yards high, and then might be seen a great stream of fire running down to the shore.[45]

Figure 41  William Dampier's views of 'burning islands' as he sailed past the northern coast of Papua New Guinea. The steep-sided volcanic island in panel no. 3 is thought to be the Ritter volcano. From Dampier's *A voyage to New Holland, &c. in the year 1699*. Oxford, Bodleian Library, 8° S 43 Jur. Vol III, part 2, opp. Table XIII.

This dramatic description could be that of a small pyroclastic flow (hot, dense clouds of pumice and ash) rushing down the mountain like a hot avalanche, formed by the collapse of the eruption column in the same way as the flows that caused such destruction at Pompeii, St Vincent and many other volcanic sites. It is likely that this description is of Ritter volcano. There are few records of its subsequent activity until 1888, when it collapsed without warning in a huge submarine landslide. There was no eruption, but tsunamis triggered by the collapse swept the nearby coastlines of

Table XIII   Dampiers Passage and Islands on $y^e$ Coast of N. Guinea

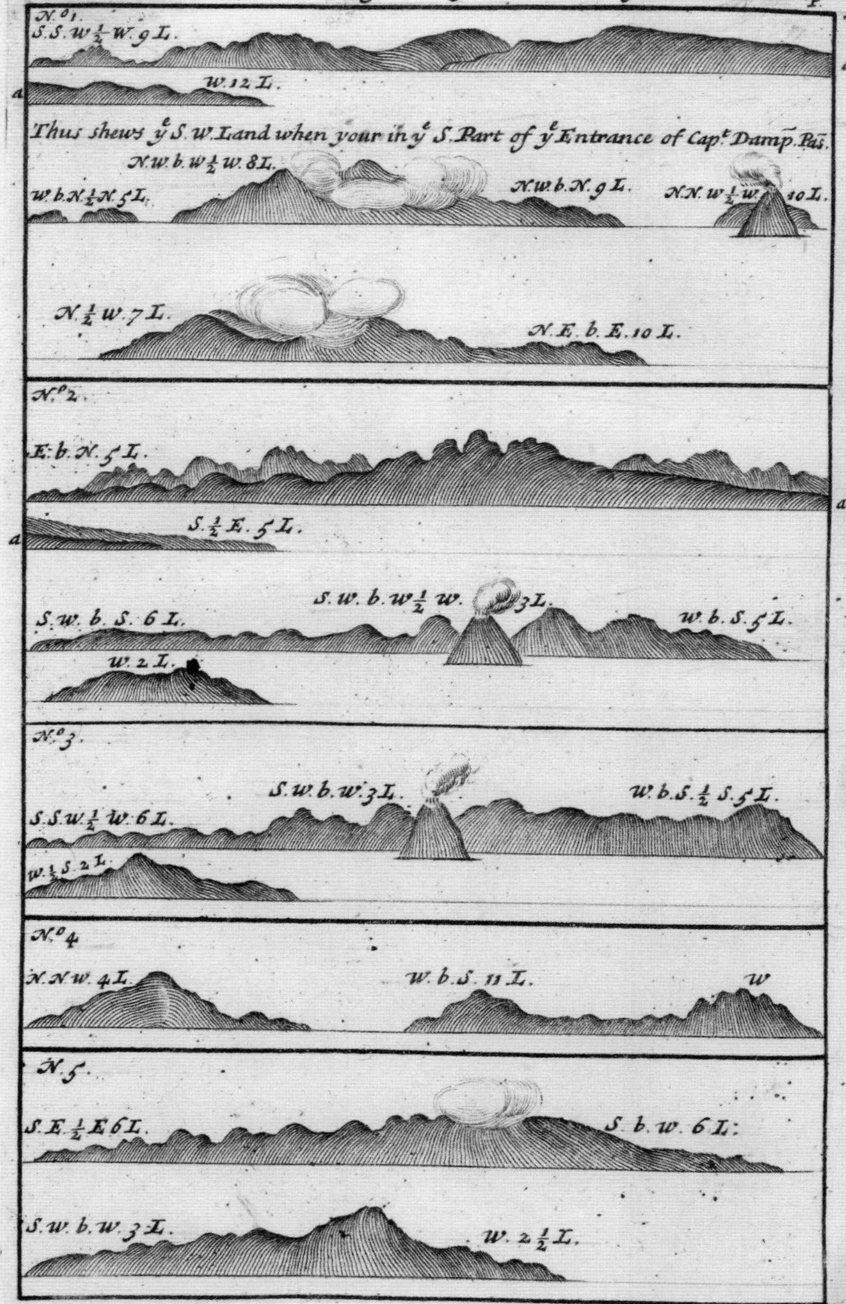

N.º 1
S.S.W. ½ W. 9 L.                                                      a
a          W. 12 L.

Thus shews $y^e$ S. W. Land when your in $y^e$ S. Part of $y^e$ Entrance of Cap.$^t$ Damp. Pas.
N.w. b. W. ½ W. 8 L.
W. b. N. ¼ N. 5 L.                    N.w. b. N. 9 L.        N.N.w. ½ w. 10 L.

N. ½ w. 7 L.                                        N.E. b. E. 10 L.

N.º 2

E. b. N. 5 L.                                                        a
a          S. ½ E. 5 L.

S.w. b. S. 6 L.        S.w. b. w. ½ w.   3 L.        w. b. S. 5 L.
W. 2 L.

N.º 3

S.w. b. w. 3 L.              w. b. S. ½ S. 5 L.
S.S.w. ½ W. 6 L.
w. ½ S. 2 L.

N.º 4

N.N.w. 4 L.              w. b. S. 11 L.                          w

N. 5

S.E. ½ E. 6 L.                                  S. b. w. 6 L.

S.w. b. w. 3 L.                          w. 2 ½ L.

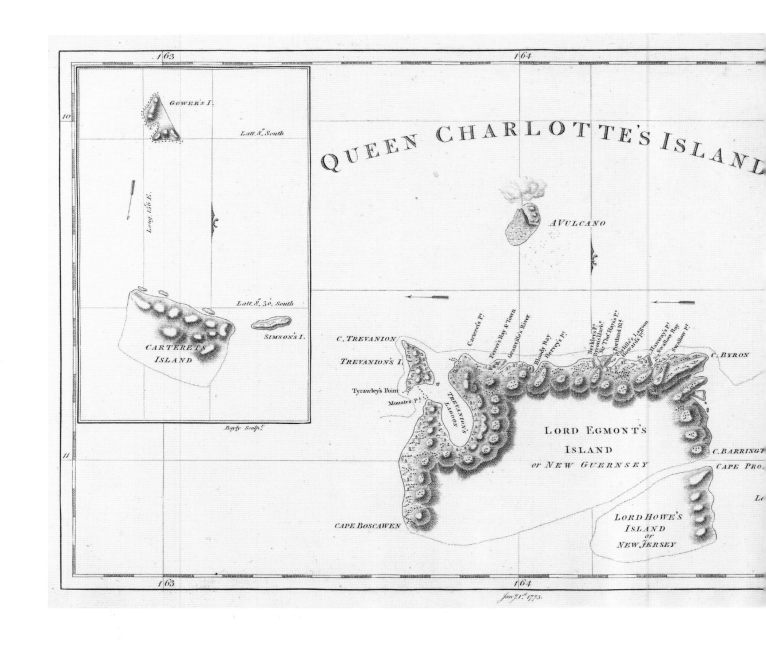

QUEEN CHARLOTTE'S ISLAND

163 · 164

10

GOWER'S I.

Latt. 8° South

Long. 159 E.

Latt. 8°.30. South

SIMSON'S I.

CARTERET'S
ISLAND

A VULCANO

C. TREVANION

TREVANION'S I.

Tyrawley's Point

Mouate's Pt.

Bayly Sculp.t

Carteret's Pt.

Ferrers Bay & Town

Granville's River

Bloody Bay

Hervey's Pt.

Berkley's Pt.

Byron's Harb.r

Sir Tho.s Hay's Pt.

Portland Isl.d

Public's Lagoon

Howard's Lagoon

Maurey's Pt.

Swallow Bay

Swallow Pt.

C. BYRON

TREVANION'S
LAGOON

LORD EGMONT'S
ISLAND
or NEW GUERNSEY

C. BARRINGT.

CAPE PRO.

CAPE BOSCAWEN

LORD HOWE'S
ISLAND
or
NEW JERSEY

11

163 · 164

Jan.y 1.st 1773.

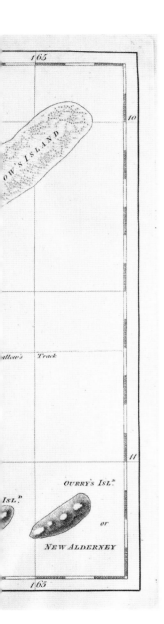

New Guinea and New Britain, causing much damage and loss of life. All that remains of the original cone of Ritter is an arcuate crescent, with a scalloped landslide scar.

## Eighteenth-century explorers

By the eighteenth century, European explorers were being sent out to travel the world to gather scientific knowledge to be shared between nations. In 1766, Philip Carteret sailed across the Pacific Ocean in the *Swallow*, passing the erupting volcano of Tinakula (Figure 42) in the present-day Solomon Islands, and the smoking volcano of Tavurvur near Rabaul, Papua New Guinea. In 1768, Captain James Cook set sail in the *Endeavour*, to observe the transit of Venus across the Sun on 3 June 1769. His was but one of many coordinated experiments planned around the globe, with the ambition of measuring the distance from the Earth to the Sun. In addition, Cook was charged with exploring the southern latitudes of the world's oceans, to see if there was another continent waiting to be discovered. Cook's first voyage was such a success that he launched two more.

The second, from 1772 to 1775, was an epic circumnavigation of the southern oceans in the *Resolution*, which revealed that the rumoured continent did not exist. Cook was accompanied by Johann Forster, a naturalist, and his son George. On the way, Forster made observations of the extinct volcanic peaks of Tahiti and Easter Island, and sailed by the young volcano of Tofua, in Tonga. On Tanna Island, in Vanuatu, he witnessed a spectacular eruption of Yasur volcano:

Figure 42 Map of Nendo, or Santa Cruz, visited by Captain Carteret in 1767, showing 'a vulcano'. The volcano is Tinakula, in the Solomon Islands. Tinakula has been frequently active since at least the sixteenth century. In 1840, pyroclastic flows killed all the inhabitants of the island. From Hawkesworth's *An account of the voyages & c.*, 1770. Oxford, Bodleian Library, Arch.Antiq. B II.30.

> Every four or five minutes we perceived a strait column of smoke, of
> a reddish-grey cast, rising with great velocity and violence; and soon
> after we heard a rumbling noise in the volcano like that of thunder.
> After the smoke, or rather mass of ignited ashes, had risen to a
> considerable height the resistance of the air, and its own gravitation,
> brought it down: it varied from the columnar shape, and branched out
> into separate masses, assuming a surface and outline not unlike a large
> cauliflower.[46]

Yasur remains in eruption today, a persistently active volcano with frequent
Strombolian and Vulcanian explosions from its central pit crater. Cook's third
expedition, again on the *Resolution*, began with an exploration of the North Pacific
Ocean and ended after his arrival at Hawaii in 1779.

The French and Spanish also launched grand expeditions to the new continent of
South America in the pursuit of science in the late eighteenth century. Don Antonio de
Ulloa, a Spanish explorer, astronomer and later governor of Louisiana, joined the French
Geodesic Mission to present-day Ecuador from 1735 to 1744. The aim of the mission was
to make very careful topographical measurements at the equator, to help to determine
the precise shape of the Earth. In Quito, they climbed to the highest summit of
Pichincha, where they stayed for twenty-three days. During their travels, they observed
a catastrophic eruption of Cotopaxi:

> In 1743, there was a new eruption, that started after a few days of
> continual rumbling in its bowels. A vent opened in the summit, and
> three others at about the same height on the snowy slopes, and ejected
> large quantities of ash that mixed with a prodigious quantity of ice and
> snow, melting amidst the flames, and that flooded in an instant the
> plain from Callo to Latacunga and formed a sea of muddy waves.[47]

This eruption, and the volcanic mudflows or lahars, caused great destruction and
considerable loss of life. Lahars remain a potent threat at ice-clad volcanoes such as
Cotopaxi. In 1877, another eruption at the same volcano fed mudflows that travelled

over 300 kilometres into the Pacific Ocean. In November 1985, mudflows formed in a similar way during an eruption of Nevado del Ruiz, Colombia, inundating the nearby town of Armero and killing over 23,000 people.

Antonio de Ulloa and his travelling companions, the French astronomers Charles Marie de La Condamine and Pierre Bouguer, wrote extensively of their expedition and their many observations (Figure 43). Bouguer's name lives on in the measurement of the Earth's gravity field, while Ulloa gave his name to the optical 'fog bow' effect, which he was the first to describe and measure.

Figure 43   Cotopaxi volcano in eruption in 1743 and the 'fog bow' first described by Antonio de Ulloa. From Ulloa's *Voyage to South America*, 1758. Oxford, Bodleian Library, Vet. A5 e.271, vol. 1, plate 5.

## Nineteenth-century natural historians

The nineteenth century saw an explosion in the exploration, documentation and the careful organization of systematic knowledge about the natural world, as well as in the development of the theories about 'how the Earth works' that help to underpin our current understanding of the Earth. In the realm of volcanoes and volcanic studies, a number of important arguments about the nature of volcanoes and volcanic heat were eventually resolved, and several significant eruptions – notably those of Santorini in 1866–71 and Krakatau in 1883 – stimulated scientific studies of volcanic processes which were remarkable for their breadth, and which helped to develop new ideas about how volcanoes behave.

To British audiences, Charles Darwin is probably the best-known natural scientist of this era. Nowadays, he is invariably linked primarily with his theory of natural selection – or evolution. But Darwin spent quite a lot of his time as an undergraduate studying geology, and many of the observations that he made during the voyage of the *Beagle* have subsequently proved to be important in the history of geology as a discipline. When Darwin joined the *Beagle* mission in September 1831 he had only recently completed his studies, and he joined 'not as a finished Naturalist, but as amply qualified for collecting, observing, & noting any thing worthy to be noted in Natural History'.[48] To help him in his endeavours, Darwin took several important books relevant to volcanoes: Alexander von Humboldt's *Personal narrative of travels to the equinoctial regions of the New Continent'* (Figure 44), which had recently been translated into English by Maria Williams; Charles Daubeny's *Description of Extinct and Active Volcanoes*; and George Poulett Scrope's *Considerations on volcanos*. Each of these books has helped shape the ways in which we think about volcanoes today, even though they are rather different in style and scope.

Alexander von Humboldt was passionately interested in the natural history of the world and set off from Europe in 1799 with the botanist Aimé Bonpland, 'to examine the interior of the new continent', South America, and to develop a 'theory of the Earth'.[49] His expedition took him thousands of kilometres across country, by foot and boat, from the volcanic plains of Mexico – where he visited the great volcano of Jorullo that had appeared out of nowhere in 1759 (see Chapter 5) – to the high volcanic mountains of present-day Ecuador and Colombia. He collected a vast amount of material and made thousands of observations of everything from atmospheric pressure to plants, animals, rocks and soils. After Humboldt returned to Europe in 1804, he was furiously prolific, and his writings on natural history, and the wonderful scientific illustrations that he used to augment them, became well known.

Humboldt's travels were scientific expeditions on a grand scale – with all the latest equipment for measuring altitude and location; the composition and properties of the atmosphere; and for botanical and geological sampling. He lists nearly fifty scientific instruments that he carried with him, including telescopes, sextants, chronometers, thermometers and barometers. He climbed many of the highest volcanoes in the world – making it much of the way up Cotopaxi and to over 19,000 feet on Chimborazo. It was after descending from his attempt on Chimborazo that Humboldt came up with the design of his signature infographic, the 'naturgemalde', which depicted in intricate detail the physical and biological structure of this giant volcanic massif.

Charles Daubeny was a professor of chemistry (and later, botany and rural economy) in the University of Oxford in the early 1800s. He was introduced to geology by William Buckland, a charismatic lecturer in geology at the university. In his quest to find out more about volcanoes and volcanic rocks, Daubeny travelled widely across Europe, visiting volcanic areas from Hungary to Sicily, and in 1826 wrote *A description of active and extinct volcanos, with remarks on their origin, their chemical phenomena and the character of their products*. Accompanying this, he published a splendid *Tabular view of volcanic phenomena*, that was a pictorial summary of the world's volcanoes and their historical activity (Figure 45). His stated ambition was to fill a gap in the market, 'no treatise on volcanoes having appeared in [English] since Ordinaire, except indeed the recent publication of Mr Poulett Scrope'.[50]

Daubeny's book is indeed wide-ranging and after an exhaustive tour of volcanoes that he had visited, or that others had written about, Daubeny turned his attention to the cause of volcanic action. This, he was careful to point out, had to be based on conjecture rather than direct observation – for all the processes that he was considering could only be deduced from their remote consequences. This constraint still holds today: it is much easier to observe the consequences of an eruption than to peer inside the volcanic source.

| ECHELLE en METRES | REFRACTION et sur la hauteur exprimée en secondes de la distance en faisant abstraction de la Température 0° | DISTANCE à laquelle les Montagnes sont visibles sur mer, en faisant abstraction de la réfraction. | HAUTEURS MESURÉES en différentes parties DU GLOBE. | PHÉNOMÈNES ÉLECTRIQUES selon la hauteur des Couches. | CULTURE DU SOL selon son élévation au-dessus du Niveau de la Mer. | DÉCROISSEMENT de la Gravitation exprimé par les oscillations d'un même Pendule dans le Vide. | ASPECT du Ciel azuré exprimé en degrés du Cyanomètre. | DÉCROISSEMENT de l'Humidité de l'Air exprimé en Degrés de l'Hygromètre de Saussure. | PRESSION de l'Air Atmosphérique exprimée en chant Barométriques. | ECHELLE en TOISES |
|---|---|---|---|---|---|---|---|---|---|---|
| | | | Élévation des petits nuages (cirrus) | | | | | | | 4,000 |
| | | | | | | | | | Bar. 0m.3008 (133.16) à 5500m. de haut. Temp. supp.° 28° | |
| | | | | | | 3482,9635 à 5000m | | | | 3,500 |
| 6000 | 90°.7 | 2′.7630 | Cime de Chimborazo 6544m (3353t) où s'observent le barométre au niveau de l'Océan par la formule barométrique de M. Laplace. | Beaucoup de Phénomènes lumineux. | | | Manque d'observations. La Sécheresse de l'air y sera maigre et probablement au-dessous de 38m par évident la Température de −15°.3 | | Bar. 0m.3235 (133.38) à 6200m de haut. Temp. supp.° 28° | |
| | | | Cime de Cayambe 5064m (3088t) | Peu d'explosions accompagnée de tonnerre. La grandeur chevauche de l'air et la proximité des nuages rendant le croissement l'Électricité très sensible. | | 3490,5404 à 5000m | | | Bar. 0m.3097 (143.4) à 5500m de haut. Temp. supp.° 30° | 3,000 |
| 5500 | | 2′.6450 | Cime d'Antisana 5833m (2993t) Cime de Cotopaxi 5753m (2952t) | | | | de 42° à 46° Intensité moyenne de 44° | sont 26°.7 | Bar. 0m.3206 (147.5) à 5500m de haut. Temp. supp.° 3.0 | |
| | | | Cime de Mont St. Elie 5865m (2810t) | | | | | | | |
| | | | Cime de Popocatepetl 5387m (2764t) | | | | | | | |
| | | | Cime du Pic d'Orizava 5205m (2717t) | | | | | | | |
| 5000 | 102°.2 | 2′.5470 | Volcan de Tunguragua 5088m (2641t) | | | 3497,1970 à 5000m | | | Bar. 0m.2823 (163.90) à 5000m de haut. Temp. supp.° 6.4 | 2,500 |
| | | | Cime de Ruca-Pichincha 4768m (2446t) Mont-Blanc 4775m (2450t) | Près du bord des Glaces elle passe souvent du positif au négatif. | Plus de Culture. Pâturages des Lamas, des Brebis, des Bœufs et des Chèvres. | | de 45° à 46° Intensité moyenne de 55° | Humidité moyenne 84° | Bar. 0m.2823 (163.90) à 5000m de haut. | |
| 4500 | | 2′.393o | Pinchevaben 4561m (2338t) Coquilles pétrifiées à Huancavelica à 4300m (2206t) | Abondance de grêle. | | | de 45° à 46° Intensité moyenne 85° | | Bar. 0m.2433 (187.35) à 4500m de haut. | |
| 4000 | 117°.0 | 2′.2860 | Mesure d'Antisana Kokoko 4016m (2208t) Gross-Glokner (in Tyrol) 3498m (1795t) | | Abondance de grêle. | 3503,8536 à 5000m | | | Bar. 0m.2457 (213.7) à 4000m de haut. Temp. supp.° 6.4 | 2,000 |
| 3500 | | 2′.1100 | Ville de Micuipampa 3555m (1826t) Mont-Perdu 3436m (1763t) Etna 3335m (1712t) | Explosions très fréquentes, mais peu d'allongé. Les Couches d'air voisine de la terre et proue long temps chargés d'Électricité négative. | Pomme de terre. Oliven. Tropæolum esculentum. Pas de Froment au-delà de 3300m | | de 63° à 57° Intensité moyenne de 52° | Humidité moyenne 69° | Bar. 0m.2496 (221.8) à 3500m de haut. Temp. supp.° 76° | |
| 3000 | 130°.5 | 1′.9540 | Wittinam 2941m (1509t) Canigou 2786m (1427t) S. Gothard Cime de Pelouse 2722m (1392t) | | Blede d'Europe Frumen. Hordeum Avena. Chenopodium. | 3495.2392 à 5000m | | de 52° à 53° | de 54° à 105° | Bar. 0m.3089 (233t 00t) à 3000m de haut. Temp. supp.° 86° | 1,500 |
| | | 1′.7840 | Limite inférieure des neiges sous la 45° de lat à 2460m de hauteur. | Depuis 3900m la grêle cesse de se montrer. | Seigle. Noyer. Pistache. Coton. En pays des Incas Juglans. Pommes | | Intensité moyenne de 55° | Humidité moyenne 74° | Bar. 0m.3023 (233.63) à 2500m de haut. Temp. supp.° 87° | |
| 2500 | | | Couche de Sel gemme de St. Maure en Savoie 2332m (1198t) Passage du Mont Cenis 2068m (1061t) | | et de Rochers (sic simo) | 3496,8468 à 5000m | | | | |
| 2000 | 149°.4 | 1′.5960 | Mont d'Or 1886m (968t) | Explosions électriques très fréquentes en hiver, elles se forment au-dessous de 1760m. L'Homme dénué difficilement deux à trois mois | Caffé, Coton, Canne à sucre même abon-dante. Au-dessous de 1760m L'Homme dénué difficilement deux à trois mois | | de 62°, à 102° Intensité moyenne de 22° | Humidité moyenne 88° | Bar. 0m.6034 (233.88) à 2000m de haut. Temp. supp.° 25° | 1,000 |
| 1500 | | 1′.3820 | Ville de Popayan 1766m (906t) Puy de Dome 1477m (758t) | | | | de 57° à 57° Intensité moyenne de 22° | | Bar. 0m.6334 (252.7) à 1500m de haut. Temp. supp.° 23° | |
| 1000 | 167°.7 | 1′.1280 | Vésine 1198m (615t) en 1793, même 930m (477t) en 1808. Brocken mit der 1063m (545t) Cabane d'Holle 1102m (520t) | Explosions électriques très fréquentes où la campagne ou vers la soirée. Pendant plus de la moitié du jour l'Électricité est libre en été, au-dessus de la limite de l'Électricité introduite par les peuples civilisé de l'Europe. | Erythroxylum peruvianum. Bolivien. Sucre, Indigo, Cacao, Caffé, Coton, Mays, Jatropha. Bananier. Vigne, Arbres Manioc (Excudere Africaine) introduit par les peuples civilisé de l'Europe. | 3493,5234 à 5000m | | de 58° à 55° Intensité moyenne de 58° | Humidité moyenne 88° | Bar. 0m.6793 (300t.00t) à 1000m de haut. Temp. supp.° 20° | 500 |
| 500 | | 0′.7980 | Kimballa, une des hautes Montagnes de la Suède 306m (157t) | | | | de 58° à 55° Intensité moyenne de 58° | Humidité moyenne 86° | Bar. 0m.7203 (316t 03t) à 500m de haut. Temp. supp.° 20° | |
| 0 | 189°.6 | 0′.0000 | | | | 3490,0003 à 5000m | | | Bar. 0m.7623 (337t. 8o t) au niveau de la Mer Temp. supp.° 15.3 | 0 |
| 500 | | | | | | | | | Tous ces degrés Hygrométriques sont exprimés par la Température moyenne correspondante à l'Échelle thermométrique. | 500 |

# GÉOGRAPHIE DES PL...

*Tableau physique ...*

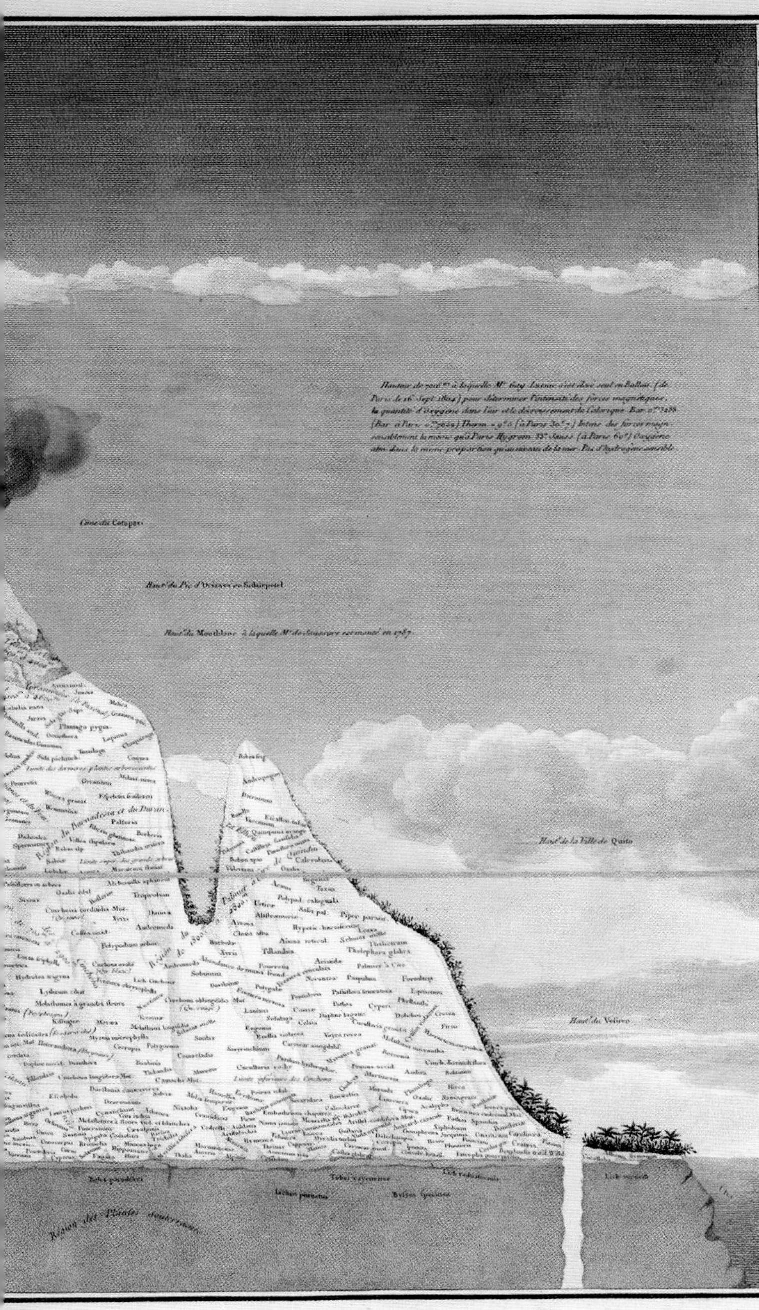


| ÉCHELLE en MÈTRES. | TEMPÉRATURE de l'Air à diverses hauteurs, exprimée en maximum et minimum du Thermomètre centigrade. | COMPOSITION CHIMIQUE de l'Air atmosphérique. | HAUTEUR de la limite inférieure de la Neige perpétuelle sous différentes latitudes. | ÉCHELLE des Animaux selon la hauteur du sol qu'ils habitent. | DEGRÉS de l'eau bouillante à différentes hauteurs. Thermomètre centigrade. | VUES Géologiques | INTENSITÉ de la Lumière dans l'air à diverses hauteurs exprimée pour unité : son intensité à dans le Vide | ÉCHELLE en TOISES. |
|---|---|---|---|---|---|---|---|---|
| 6500 | | | | Pas d'Etres organisés fixés au Sol. | Eau bouillante à 77°,0 (61°,6 R) Bar. 0m 320. | La nature des Roches paraît en général indépendante des différences de latitude et de hauteur. Mais en ne considérant qu'une petite partie du Globe, on découvre que dans chaque région l'ordre de superposition des roches, l'inclinaison et la direction de leurs couches ont été déterminées par un système de forces particulier. On reconnaît qu'il existe de certaines lois locales selon lesquelles s'élèvent les différentes formations au dessus du niveau de la mer.<br>Les Régions équatoriales présentent à la fois les cimes les plus élevées et les plaines les plus étendues du Globe depuis 0° à 1° 45' et nulle part ailleurs sur la terre, les montagnes excèdent la hauteur de 5850m. Leur abaissement vers les pôles n'est cependant pas très considérable ; car sous les 19°, les 45° et les 60° de latitude bor. on a trouvé des Cimes de 4700m et même de 5500m d'élévation.<br>Les Plaines équatoriales au contraire, celles contenues entre la pente orientale des Andes et les côtes du Brésil, sur 700 lieues de long, n'ont pas 70m à 100m de hauteur au dessus du niveau de l'Océan.<br>Toutes les formations que l'on a découvertes sur le reste du Globe, se trouvent réunies sous l'Equateur. Leur ancienneté relative, qui se manifeste dans l'ordre de leur superposition, y paraît en général la même que dans les Zones tempérées. Les granites, qui servent de base au Gneiss, au Syenite, au Schiste micacé et au Schiste primitif, les formations secondaires, deux de grès, deux de Gypse et trois de Roches calcaires, offrent des exemples frappants de l'identité de structure qui règne dans les parties les plus éloignées du Globe. La formation problématique des Basaltes, des Amygdaloïdes, des Roches amphiboliques et des Porphyres à base d'Obsidienne et de Pierre perlée (Perlstein) se trouve éparse sur la haute crête des Andes, comme elle l'est sur celle des hautes chaînes de l'Europe.<br>Parmi les phénomènes géologiques qui sont particuliers aux Régions équatoriales du nouveau Continent, on doit citer sur tout l'épaisseur des couches et la grande hauteur à laquelle on découvre les formations postérieures au Granite. En Europe le Granite n'est pas couvert par d'autres Roches depuis 3300m à 4700m. Aux Andes on ne le voit pas au dessus de 3500m. Les Cimes les plus élevées du Globe sont d'un Porphyre dans lequel l'Amphibole abonde qui est dépourvu de Quarz et que quelques Minéralogistes regardent comme produit. D'autres [illegible] formations de Grès se trouvent à Huancavelica à 4500m. Le Charbon de terre se découvre près de Huanuco à 4400m de hauteur. Les plaines de Bogota, à 2700m et 2900m sont couvertes de Grès, de Pierres calcaires secondaires, de Gypse et de Sel gemme. Des Coquilles pétrifiées se trouvent aux Andes au dessus de 4200m (en Europe on ne les a pas vu au dessus de 3500m.)<br>Le Sol du Royaume de Quito contient à 2500m de hauteur d'énormes ossemens d'Eléphants dont l'espèce paraît détruite.<br>Les Grès de Cuenca ont 1560m d'épaisseur ; une formation de Quarz à l'Ouest de Caxamarca en a 2900m.<br>La Cordillère des Andes présente plus de 50 Volcans enflammés dont quelques uns sont éloignés de la mer de 37 à 40 lieues marines et dont les plus élevés et les plus renfoncés par les flancs ne vomissent pas de laves coulantes, mais des Pierres ponces, des Obsidiennes, des Porphyres et des Basaltes scorifiés, et sur tout de l'Eau et cette terre carbonée dans laquelle est souvent enveloppé un poisson (le Pimelodus Cyclopum) | 0,9164 | 3500t |
| 6000<br>5500 | Régions trop peu fréquentées pour en connaître la Température moyenne, qui cependant y paraît être au dessous de zéro. A 5403m le Thermomètre monte quelquefois à 1°,8. | La quantité d'oxygène atmosphérique paraît la même dans les hautes régions et dans les plaines. | L'air retiré de l'eau de Neige contient 0,287 d'Oxigène. | Le Condor des Andes, quelques mouches et Sphinx voltigeant dans les airs, peut-être élevés en ces Régions par les courans ascendans | Eau bouillante à 81°,0 (64°,8 R) Bar. 0m 367. | | 0,9047 | 3000 |
| 5000<br>4500 | de 7°,5 à 18°,7 Température moyenne 3,7 (3° R.) Il tombe de la neige jusqu'à 4100m. | Mais la proximité des Volcans peut quelquefois, sur les hautes Cimes des Andes, modifier la composition de l'air. | Neige perpét. sous l'Equateur et de 3° lat. bor. à 3° lat. australe 4800m (2464t) Pas de variations de 60m. Neige perpétuelle sous les 20° latit. bor. à 4600m (2361t) mais elle y descend en hiver à 3800m | Des Vigognes, des Guanaco, des Alpaca en bandes nombreuses. Quelques Ours. Condor. Faucons Caprimulgue. Plus de poissons dans les lacs. | Eau bouillante à 84°,7 (67°,7 R) Bar. 0m 418. | | 0,8922 | 2500 |
| 4000<br>3500 | de 0° à 20° Température moyenne 9° (7°,2 R.) Abondance de grêle, même quelquefois de nuit. | La quantité d'hydrogène contenue dans l'air atmosphérique est moindre de deux millièmes. On ne trouve pas plus d'hydrogène à 7000m d'élévation qu'au niveau de la mer. | Neige perpétuelle sous les 35° de latitude à 3500m (1800t) de hauteur.<br>Neige perpétuelle sous les 42° de lat. à 3100m (1600t) de hauteur. | Des Lama devenus sauvages à la pente occidentale du Chimborazo. Le petit Ours à front blanc. Grands Cerfs. Le petit Lion. Quelques Colibri. Plus de pasteurs pénétrans | Eau bouillante à 88° (70°,5 R) Bar. 0m 474. | | 0,8787 | 2000 |
| 3000<br>2500 | de 1°,2 à 23°,7 Température moyenne 18°,7 (15° R.) Grêle très abondante. Brume fréquente en peu élevée. | | Neige perpétuelle sous les 45° de latitude bor. à 2500m (1282t) Aux Pyrénées à 2440m En Suisse à 2700m sur les Cimes isolées ; à 2530m si la cime des Montagnes dépasse 3100m. Phénomènes peu constans dans les Zones variables. | Viverra mapurito. Felis tigrina. Grands Cerfs. Palamedea bispinosa. Abondance de Canards et de Plongeurs. Beaucoup de poux. (Ped. Hum.) | Eau bouillante à 91°,3 (73°,0 R) Bar. 0m 536. | | 0,8640 | 1500 |
| 2000<br>1500 | de 12°,5 à 30° Température moyenne 21°,2 (17° R.) Grêle assez rare. Ciel souvent brumeux. | L'air atmosphérique contient 0,210 d'oxygène, 0,787 d'Azote et environ 0,003 d'Acide carbonique. Le maximum de ses variations ne paraît pas excéder un millième d'oxygène. | Sous l'Equateur on voit tomber de la neige à 4100m (2100t) de hauteur. Au Méxique sous le 19° de latitude elle tombe jusqu'à 1800m de hauteur. | Petits Cerfs (Cervus mexic.) Tapir. Sus Tajassou. Felis pardalis. Quelques Singes Alouates. Troupial (Oriolus) Coluber coccin. Pas de Boa, pas de Crocodile. Beaucoup de Chiques (Pul. penet.) | Eau bouillante à 94°,3 (75°,4 R) Bar. 0m 605. | | 0,8478 | 1000 |
| 1000<br>500 | de 18°,5 à 38°,4 Température moyenne 25,3 (20°,2 R.) Pas de Grêle. Le sable souvent à 52°. | | Neige perpétuelle sous les 75° de latitude bor. | Singes Sapajou et Alouates. Jaguar (Felis onca) Tigre noir. Lion (Felis concolor) Cavia capibara. Paresseux. Fourmilier. Cormorant. Armadille. Aptenodytes. Crax. Ampelis. Boa. Crocodile. Lamantin. Elater noctil. Mosquito (Oestr. Human.) | Eau bouillante à 97°,1 (77°,7) Bar. 0m 679. | | 0,8309 | 500 |
| 0<br>500 | L'eau de mer à la surface près de l'Equateur hors des courans à 28° mais à la profondeur de 400m la mer est à 7°,6. La Temp. de l'intérieur du Globe paraît sous l'Equat. de 22°,3. | | | Dans l'intérieur du Globe de nouvelles espèces de Dermestes qui rongent les plantes souterraines. | Eau bouillante à 100° (80 R) Bar. 0m 762. | | 0,8123 | 0 |
| | | | | | | | | 500 |

# NTES ÉQUINOXIALES.

*Andes et Pays voisins*

A Tabular View
OF
VOLCANIC PHÆNOMENA
Comprising
A LIST OF THE BURNING MOUNTAINS
That have been noticed at any time since the commencement of
Historical records or which appear to have existed at
antecedent periods,
together with
THE DATES OF THEIR RESPECTIVE ERUPTIONS,
and of the
Principal Earthquakes
connected with them

BY CHARLES DAUBENY, M.D. F.R.S.

*Professor of Chemistry in the University of Oxford &c.
intended as a companion to the Description of active and extinct Volcanos
lately Published by the same Author.*

PUBLISHED BY J. VINCENT OXFORD & W. PHILLIPS LONDON.

J. & J. Neele sc. 352 Strand.

VIE
COMPARATIVE HEIGH

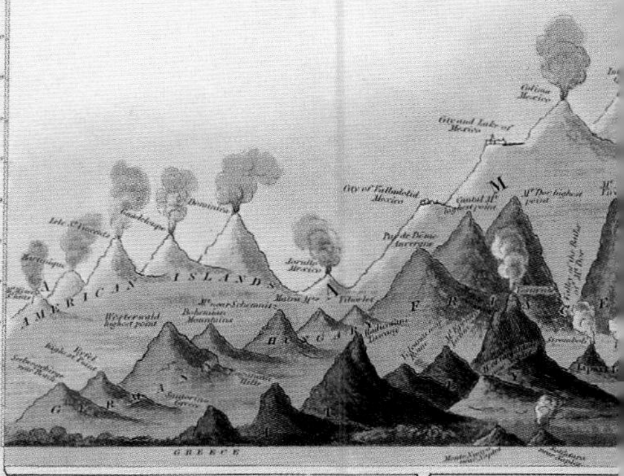

EUROPE

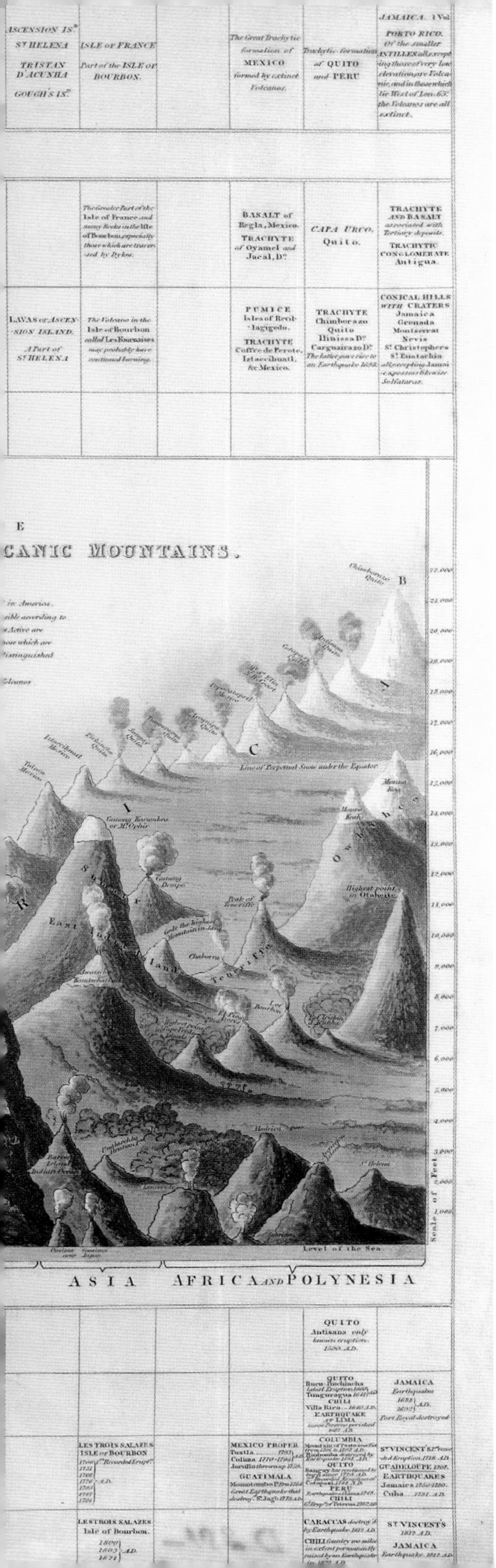

A number of the theories of volcanoes at that time suggested that the heat, or combustion, seen in eruptions was released by chemical activity. Suggestions included the spontaneous combustion of sulphur, coal or petroleum, or of metals or metal salts inside the Earth. Daubeny argued that although burning sulphur, oil or coal might explain the heat and the association of sulphur gases with volcanoes, it couldn't explain why volcanoes would erupt lavas that were so different from the material that was burning. On the other hand, the idea that volcanic activity might be due to heat released by the reaction of metals with water seemed to have quite a lot going for it. Many of the known volcanoes at that time (Daubeny counted 163) lay close to the sea, and those that did not were often parts of volcanic chains that might eventually reach the sea.

George Poulett Scrope, writing at about the same time, had also noted a general link between water and volcanism. His interest in volcanoes had begun with a trip to Italy when he was still a student and had seen Vesuvius 'then in permanent eruption' in the winter of 1817/18. The next year he toured Etna and the volcanoes of the Aeolian Islands (Stromboli and Lipari), and then, after completing his geological studies, spent six months among the extinct volcanoes of the Auvergne, Velay and Vivarais of France (Figure 46).

Figure 44 *previous page* Humboldt's 'naturgemalde', showing the distribution of plants and climate zones in the equatorial regions, with a backdrop of the Chimborazo and Cotopaxi volcanoes. Alexander von Humboldt, *Essai sur la géographie des plantes*, 1805. Oxford, Bodleian Library, Hist. a.48.

Figure 45 Charles Daubeny's chart of the comparative heights of volcanic mountains, 1827. Oxford, Bodleian Library, (E) B1 (585).

He returned to Vesuvius 'in time to witness the stupendous eruption of October 1822',[51] which he sketched and used as a frontispiece for his grandly titled book *Considerations on Volcanos, the probable causes of their phenomena, the laws which determine their march, the disposition of their products, and their connexion with the present state and past history of the globe, leading to the establishment of A New Theory of the Earth* (see Figure 10).

In developing his theory of volcanic action, Scrope was influenced by his own observations of lava within the summit crater of Stromboli, which contained 'a body of melted lava, alternately rising and falling within the chasm', and of the explosion of 'immense bubbles, that drive upwards a shower of liquid lava that, cooling rapidly in the air, falls in the form of scoria'.[52] This seemed to Scrope to require that volcanoes must contain a mass of boiling liquid 'of indeterminate extent and at an intense temperature',[53] as well as freely moving bubbles of gas. Scrope was also struck by the fact that most volcanic products contain crystals and are very rarely glassy, as might be expected if they had been completely molten and then frozen. To explain how magma could be mobile but crystalline, Scrope suggested that this was due to the very large quantities of steam passing through, and out of, the magma.

But where might the heat come from? Scrope was aware of observations – from mines – that the temperature inside the Earth increases with depth, and suggested that volcanoes were caused by 'the exposure of subterranean masses of crystalline rock to a continuous supply of heat from below'.[54] He reasoned further that since melting rocks causes them to expand, this heating to the liquid state would increase pressure, leading to the opening of fissures, allowing magma and steam to escape (Figure 47).

The influences of these three authors can be seen in some of Darwin's writings: his *Journal of a Voyage Round the World*, which was first published in 1842, combines travelogue with observations on the natural world in the same way that brought Humboldt success with *Personal Narrative*. His speculations on the links between coral reefs and volcanoes may well owe much to Scrope's global map of volcanoes and great mountain ranges. Daubeny's book was recommended to Darwin by Adam Sedgwick, his geology tutor at Cambridge, perhaps because of its value as a systematic reference work, in which it was rather more successful than Scrope's book.

Figure 46  Early geological map of the volcanoes of the Auvergne, from George Poulett Scrope's *Memoir on the geology of central France*, 1827. Oxford, Bodleian Library, 2 DELTA 76.

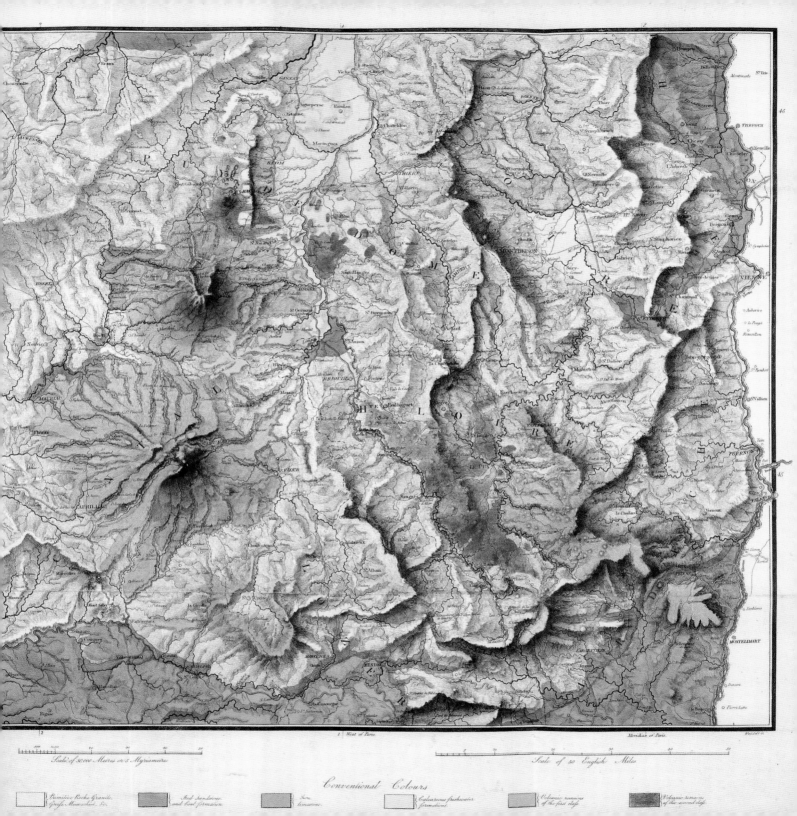

Scale of 50.000 Metres or 5 Myriametres

Scale of 50 English Miles

1 West of Paris

Meridian of Paris

The circumstances by which these alterations are produced, come now under our consideration.

§. 45. The liquefied mass (or *focus*) left by any eruption, continually abstracting caloric from the solid lava which encloses it, proportionately retards the augmentation of the expansive force of its inferior strata, which only increase in temperature as long as they are unable to part with their excess of caloric, in the ratio in which they receive it from below.

Fig 9.

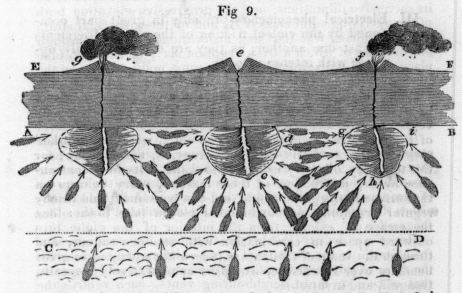

Thus, let *a b c d* be supposed the section of the liquefied lava mass, or focus, left by the eruption which produced the cone *e*, in the subterranean mass of heated lava, A B C D. *a b c d* has been reduced by ebullition to a lower temperature than the enclosing mass, and therefore abstracts caloric from it in the directions indicated by the arrows.—Consequently the inferior strata of this mass, viz. C D, part with their caloric more quickly than before the eruption.  If the vent remain permanently open, the draught of caloric thus created is regular, uniform and constant.  If the vent is shut by the predominance of the repressive force, the draught of caloric towards the focus *a b c d* takes place in a continually retarded ratio.  In the former case, the caloric may make its escape outwardly in the same ratio in which it is communicated from below to the inferior strata of the lava mass, in which conse-

Darwin's voyages on the *Beagle* took him to many volcanic islands, including St Helena, Ascension and the Galapagos, where he made some important observations on the settling out of dense crystals from lavas. In Chile, he experienced a great earthquake, which led him to ponder the links between mountains, earthquakes and volcanoes. In the Pacific, Darwin was greatly struck by the puzzle of why some islands were fringed by coral reefs, while in atolls the central island was no longer visible. His solution was that while the islands were gradually sinking, the coral reefs would grow to maintain their position at around sea level. This ingenious explanation is still the preferred interpretation today, and brings us to the longest chain of volcanoes in the Pacific Ocean – the Hawaiian archipelago.

## Hawaii

The volcanic islands of the Hawaiian archipelago stretch for over 2,400 kilometres across the Pacific Ocean. The only currently volcanically active island of this chain – the 'Big Island' of Hawaii – is home to the largest volcano on Earth, Mauna Loa, and to the most productive volcano of the past thirty years, Kilauea.

Mauna Loa is a classic shield-shaped volcano that rises to an elevation of more than 4 kilometres above sea level, and more than 9 kilometres above the ocean floor. As you travel west along the island chain, the volcanic islands become older and more deeply dissected by weathering and erosion, until little or nothing of the original island is visible above the sea. The last island of the chain, Kure Atoll, is little more than a circular reef of coral, clinging to the underwater remnants of what would have been a volcano about 30 million years ago. Underwater, the submarine 'seamounts' of the Emperor volcanic chain can be traced all the way to the edge of the Pacific Plate, offshore from Russia's far-eastern coast, more than 6,400 kilometres from Hawaii. The geological explanation of why the islands are there dates back to the early days of plate tectonic theory and an idea advanced by J. Tuzo Wilson that there was a fixed 'hot' source of molten rock within the mantle, which would supply magma to build volcanoes and then islands as the Pacific tectonic plate moved over the top. A clumsy analogy would be to imagine passing a sheet of paper over a candle, and to imagine the volcanoes tracing out the burn mark in that sheet. In the geological model, the current hot spot lies underneath Hawaii, and the small submarine volcano of Loihi marks the leading edge of the surface expression.

The Hawaiian islands were settled by Polynesians nearly 2,000 years ago, and there is a rich cultural record of the volcanism of the islands, much of it associated with Pele, the Hawaiian goddess, or *akua*, of volcanoes. In Hawaiian, Pele means lava, or eruption, and Pele is associated with the consumption of forests and land, and has inspired many ancient poems and legends, including the idea that Pele had originally lived on Kauai, but to escape, the goddess of the sea had travelled eastwards, from island to island, before finally taking up refuge in the Halemaumau crater at the summit of Kilauea volcano.

James Cook landed at Kealakekua Bay in 1778, remarking that 'Owyhee has every appearance in nature to suppose it once to have been a vulcano',[55] but there were no first-hand accounts from explorers of volcanic activity until the 1820s. Some of the earliest written records of contemporary volcanic activity in the crater of Kilauea come from travellers of the early nineteenth century.

In 1828, missionaries William Ellis and Charles Stewart published accounts of their journeys around Hawaii in June 1825, which include a description of the long hike to reach the bubbling lava lake at the summit of Kilauea's Halemaumau crater:

> The crater is an immense chasm, approached not by ascending a cone, but by descending two terraces.[56]
>
> …
>
> As the darkness of the night gathered, fire after fire began to glimmer on the eye. Two or three of the small craters nearest us were in full action, every moment casting out stones, ashes and lava with heavy detonations. The great seat of action seemed to be at the southern and western end, where an exhibition of ever varying fireworks was presented, surpassing in beauty and sublimity all that the ingenuity of art ever devised. Rivers of fire were seen rolling in splendid coruscation among the labouring craters, and on one side a lake, which surface constantly flashed and sparkled with the agitation of contending currents.[57]

Ellis and Stewart made this ascent with a party of British travellers, who had come to the 'Sandwich Islands' on HMS *Blonde* with Lord Byron, cousin of the poet. Robert Dampier sketched the same view of Kilauea crater, which was later published in a book of the expedition, written by the well-known travel writer and natural historian Maria Graham (Figure 48).

Hawaii remained a firm tourist destination from then on, attracting the attention of later travellers including Isabella Bird and Constance Gordon-Cumming. Gordon-Cumming, who was a travel writer and artist, visited Hawaii in October 1879 after a long journey across the Pacific and back on a postal steamer. Arriving in Oahu reminded her of the dark gabbro mountains of Skye and the barren volcanic coasts of Aden and the Red Sea. During her extended stay she hiked up into the mountains to see the volcanic crater at the summit of Kilauea. The crossing took them by 'long stretches of smooth, glossy, cream-coloured satin rock called pa-hoe-hoe, which looks as if a glassy river had suddenly been congealed with all of its ripples', and across 'the terrible streams of a-a, the hardest, most jagged, most cruel class of rock'.

The view afforded to Gordon-Cumming would not have been very different from that of 50 years before, and from a distance and at night she could see a 'glowing cloud rising from the fire-lake, like red hot cinders, as the only indications of the mighty power working beneath us'.[58] At sunrise, she could see across a great summit crater, paved with a floor of lava: 'At the far side of this crater lies the inner circle, which is the true chimney, and is known as Halemaumau, or house of everlasting burning (Figure 49). At present the lake of fire is enclosed by a high circle of crags, within which the awful waves of unquenchable fire surge and writhe without ceasing.'[59]

Her excitement was short-lived. After crossing a 'billowy ocean of lava waves' – and finding filmy, fine-spun tresses of volcanic glass, huge lumps of kidney iron and banks of very dark, close-grained lava, with veins of tiny sparkling green crystals of olivine – she 'climbed over coils of huge hollow vitreous lava-pipes which constantly broke beneath our weight, and at last gained the summit and looked eagerly for the Lake of Fire to find that "THERE WAS NONE"'.[60]

Only a few days had passed since her guide had watched blood-red waves dashing in scarlet spray against the cliffs, but now, little was visible but a chaos of broken-up crags looming black and awful through ever-shifting clouds of white vapour. 'We might have

been standing on Highland crags, looking down through the mists on some dark tarn. Stayed there 3 hours, sketching; in clearer moments we could see flickering flames from narrow fissures, mainly of a pale blue colour.'[61]

On her way back, they found another blowing cone or chimney – where the flow of the molten material vividly recalled the casting of big guns in the Gateshead iron-works. Just a few days later, the lava returned. On 2 November 1879, she wrote:

At this very moment, there lies before me a perfect network of rivers of molten rock which, having burst from the newly created lake, are now meandering at their own wild will over the bed of the great crater. All last night we watched the marvellous scene, fresh rivers bursting up every few minutes from one point or another. First appears a glowing spot of fire in the black lava bed, then begins a spouting. Then a pool of molten lava forms, and presently a flow commences which gradually increases until it becomes a rushing river. Today, I have stood beside rivers of fire, some rushing fully twice as fast as I could run. The bed of the inner crater has sunk out of sight; the house of everlasting burning is now a bottomless pit![62]

A little while after leaving the islands of Hawaii, there was a tremendous eruption of Mauna Loa. A fiery glow in the clouds above Mauna Loa showed that a new summit eruption was beginning:

Soon the fire flood forced an opening on the sides of the volcano, about six miles north of the summit-crater, and the fire fountains played, and very soon formed three huge cones, meanwhile the stream of lava poured downward, and after burning many hundred acres of forest and filling up all the irregularities of the ground, it formed a great lake of tossing, raging fire …[63]

Figure 48 *previous page* Robert Dampier's sketch of a view in June 1825 across the 'volcano Peli', the crater of Kilauea volcano, Hawaii. From Maria Graham's *Voyage of HMS Blonde to the Sandwich islands, in the years 1824–1825*. Oxford, Bodleian Library, 383.11 s. 1.

Figure 49  Sketch of the active vent of Halemaumau, Kilauea volcano, Hawaii, 1879. From Constance Gordon-Cumming's *Fire Fountains*, 1883. Oxford, Bodleian Library, (OC) 203 i.120, Vol 1, opp. p. 166.

Figure 50 *overleaf* The fuming vent of Halemaumau crater, Kilauea, 2008. © Tjarda Roberts

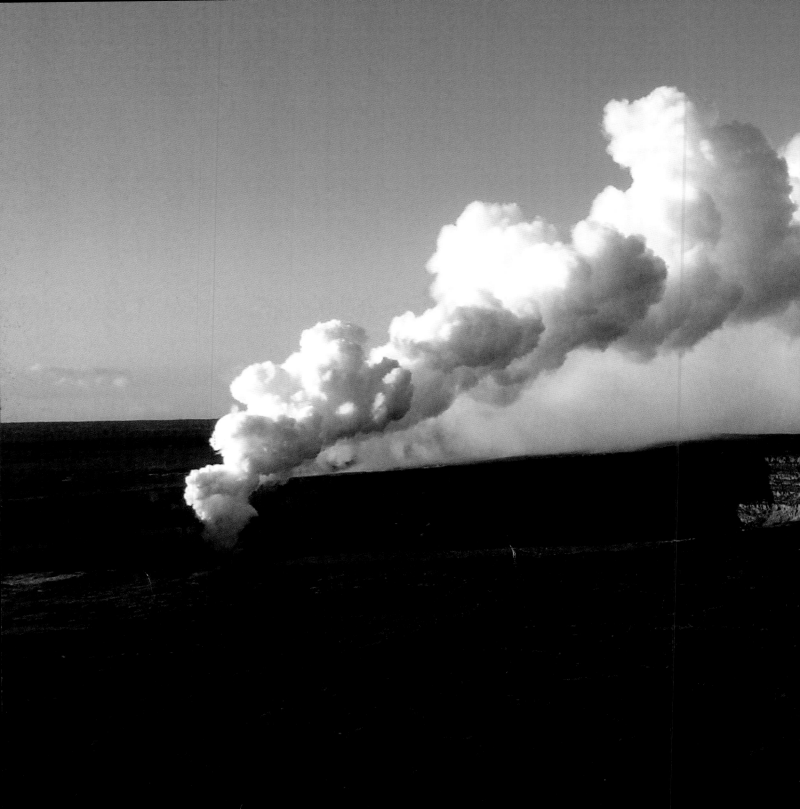

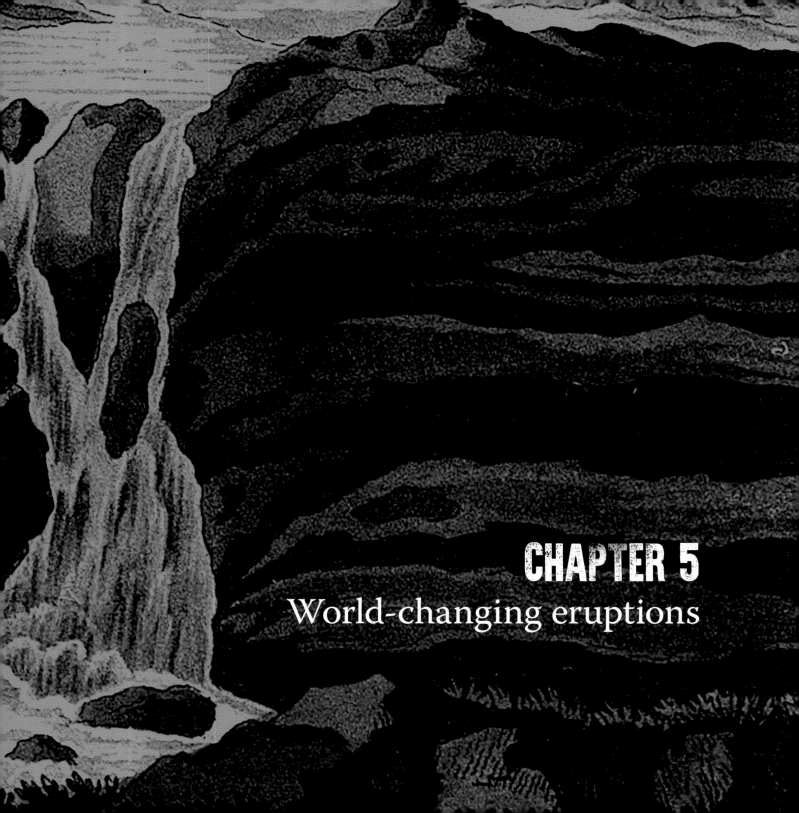

# CHAPTER 5
World-changing eruptions

VOLCANIC ERUPTIONS can have dramatic and life-changing consequences, on all scales from the local to the global. Eruptions can be large enough to change the landscape, whether by the growth or the destruction of a volcano. Volcanic eruptions at sea may create new islands or cause others to disappear. Once in a generation, volcanic eruptions may be large enough, and release enough gaseous pollutants, that they can leave an indelible mark on the Earth's climate system, with consequences that may be felt at distances far removed from the source of the eruption, through changes in weather patterns. This chapter explores historical accounts of such dramatic eruptions and their aftermath.

## Appearing and disappearing islands

In 1639 a pamphlet was published in London describing 'a true and strange relation of fire which by an eruption brake forth out of the bowels of the earth in the depths of the sea and made an island of four miles and a half in length, one of the islands of the Terceira's, to the amazement of beholders, which happened in the month of July 1638'.[64] This 'prodigious eruption of fire exhaled in the middle of the ocean', forming a new island close to the island of São Miguel, in the present-day Azores. After a week the eruption stopped, leaving great quantities of dead fish washed up on the nearby islands. The new island soon disappeared, its top washed back below sea level by the waves of the Atlantic Ocean.

It is likely that the same island reappeared in a new eruption in June 1811 (Figure 51), which was documented by James Tillard, captain of the Royal Navy ship *Sabrina*, which had recently anchored at Ponta Delgada. Initially, he thought that the columns of smoke

Figure 51 Illustration for a children's book of the 1811 eruption at Sabrina Island, near São Miguel, Azores. From Opie's *Wonders!*, 1821. Oxford, Bodleian Library, Opie H 195.

## ST. MICHAEL'S VOLCANO.

Well! this is a wonder of wonders to me!
Such volumes of fire bursting out from the sea!
With lava, and ashes, and sulphurous smell,
I'm surpris'd that the sailors can bear it so well!
Yet all must desire the eruption to view,
And if I were there I might feel anxious too.

London Published. July 2 1822. by J. Harris & Son. corner of St Pauls.

## PYRAMIDS AND SPHINX

Well, surely we need not the eye of a lynx,
The Pyramids here to discover;
Or find out the comical thing call'd "the Sphinx,"
Whose bosom is thirty feet over;
Near Memphis these wonders of art may be seen,
And there for some thousands of years they have been.

were from a fight between two ships, but it soon became clear that the scale was somewhat larger:

> Suddenly a column of the blackest cinders, ashes and stones would shoot up in form of a spire at an angle of from ten to twenty degrees from a perpendicular line … this was rapidly succeeded by a second, third, fourth, each acquiring greater velocity … until they had attained an altitude as much above the level of our eye, as the sea was below it. … [When] the ascending motion had nearly ceased, they broke into various branches resembling a group of pines, these again forming themselves into festoons of white feathery smoke.[65]

The volcanic island continued to erupt and grow, and Tillard was eventually able to land a rowing boat there on 4 July. He walked a lap of the island in twelve minutes, finding skeletons of fish and lots of 'porous substances, generally burnt to complete cinders'– volcanic scoria and ash.[66] On the highest point, Tillard planted the Union Jack, left a sealed bottle with an account of the formation of the island, named the island Sabrina and claimed it for Great Britain. Fortunately, the eruption came to an end; erosion soon reclaimed the island for the sea and a potential diplomatic incident was defused.

Similar examples of volcanic islands appearing and then disappearing again have been described from around the world. In July 1831, a new island appeared in the Mediterranean, offshore from Sicily. Graham

Figure 52 Surtsey, an eruption in progress, November 1963. Photo © Sólarfilma, Iceland.

Island – named for the then First Lord of the Admiralty – was promptly claimed by a British sailor, Captain Senhouse. Subsequently, the island was also named and claimed – Ferdinandea, for the King of the Two Sicilies, and l'île Julia, for France. The island grew to a height of 60 metres before the eruptions ceased, and within six months had disappeared again. This brief period of time nonetheless offered many opportunities for scientific exploration, and many samples of the volcanic ash and pumice found their way to museum collections around the world. Today, the island is a shallow submarine shoal, known as the Campi Flegrei Mar di Sicilia. It briefly made the news again in 1986, when it was mistaken for a submarine and bombed by a US airforce pilot who was on a sortie to Libya, and again, in 2002, when it began to show some seismic unrest.

From 1963 to 1967, the new volcanic island of Surtsey formed in the Vestmannaeyjar Islands, south of Iceland (Figure 52). The spectacular steam and ash explosions, as the erupting magma mixed with seawater, inspired the term 'surtseyan' to describe this style of eruption. Surtsey then became a laboratory to study the arrival and evolution of life on a pristine island. Late in 2014 another dramatic example of surtseyan activity led to the formation of the new island of Hunga Tonga-Hunga Ha'apai, in the South Pacific.

## Jorullo and Parícutin

The Trans-Mexican volcanic belt is one of the most extensive continental volcanic regions on Earth. It stretches 1,000 kilometres from the Pacific Ocean to the Gulf of Mexico across south–central Mexico, and is home to both long-lived volcanoes such as Popocatépetl and Volcan de Colima, and to the fabled 'pop-up' volcanoes that appeared as if out of nowhere, such as Jorullo and Parícutin.

A vast plain extends from the hills of Aguasarco in central Mexico to the villages of Teipa and Pelatlan, both celebrated for their fine plantations of cotton. Here, the fields covered with sugar cane and indigo that belonged to the farm of Don Pedro de Jorullo were among the most fertile in the country. In June 1759, a 'subterraneous noise' was heard. Hollow sounds of the most alarming nature were accompanied by frequent earthquakes, to the great consternation of the inhabitants of the farm. By the beginning of September things had quietened down, until the night of the 20th when the underground rumblings began again.

Figure 53 View of Jorullo volcano and the plain of small volcanic cones, or *hornitos*, which erupted in Mexico in 1759. From Humboldt's *Vue des Cordillères*. Wellcome Library, London.

There are no eyewitness records directly from the time, and Alexander von Humboldt was the first naturalist to visit, in 1803 (Figure 53). His investigations suggested that the eruption of Jorullo began when 'a tract of ground 3 to 4 square miles in extent rose up like a bladder'. There then followed five months of vigorous eruptions. From the main cone of what became Jorullo volcano,

> fragments of burning rocks were thrown to prodigious heights and through a thick cloud of ashes, illuminated by volcanic fire, the surface of the earth was seen to swell up like an agitated sea. Thousands of small cones, called "ovens" (hornitos) erupted across the region, and in the midst of this, six large masses sprung up from a chasm, the most elevated of which is the great volcano of Jorullo. It is continuously burning and has thrown out from its north side great quantities of scoria and basaltic lava.[67]

A few years later, George Scrope suggested that Humboldt had been misled into thinking that the volcano had been inflated like a balloon by mysterious forces inside the earth by the 'mischief-working elevation-crater hypothesis of von Buch'.[68] The 'craters of elevation' argument centred over whether volcanoes were mountains because they had been pushed up or whether they were mountains because they grew during eruptions. Other geologists had visited Jorullo and noticed the similarity between the great hornito-studded lava plains of Jorullo and similar features in the main lava-filled craters of Hawaii and Vesuvius. Scrope was familiar with ancient examples of volcanic cone-fields from his geological travels across the Auvergne (Figure 54). This suggested to Scrope that the Jorullo activity was simply a spectacular example of what we now call a 'monogenetic' basaltic eruption, where a batch of magma breaks through the crust to build a set of volcanic cones and fissure-fed lava fields. Jorullo will never erupt again, but it is just one of many similar volcanic cones and cone fields within the vast continental volcanic field – each of which is also the product of a single discrete eruption.

In the nineteenth century, Jorullo was the archetype volcano that appeared from nowhere, in very much the same way that Parícutin, 80 kilometres away, grew out of a farmer's corn field in 1943. Dionisio Pulido was the farmer, and in one of his fields there was a small depression about a metre deep. For years he would empty debris into the hole, but it never seemed to fill up, and eventually he started to use it to store things such as his yoke and plough. The day of 20 February 1943 was calm and clear, and Dionisio and his wife, Paula, noticed some deep rumbling sounds, a little like thunder. Paula was tending her sheep that day, and in mid-afternoon saw what looked like a swirling column of dust moving along the ground and a wide crack opening up. At about 4 pm there was a strong whistling noise, a smell of sulphur and more grey dust, and some pine trees near the depression in the ground burst into flames. The ground swelled and a grey dusty plume rose above the ground.

This was the start of a dramatic eruption; within a day incandescent rocks were being thrown violently out of the ground, a vigorous eruption column developed, lit up by lightning, and lava began to flow. By the time Parícutin had finished erupting, nine years later, it had grown a volcanic cone over 400 metres high and covered 25 square kilometres of land with lava. For those eking out a living on the land around the volcano, the eruption caused significant disruption. For the first two months, large quantities of ash and cinders affected the villages and fields closest to the new volcano. When the seasonal rains arrived in May, there was a terrible 'rain of mud'. People fled the eruption temporarily, but came back to their lands once the activity had begun to settle down. For the next few months, life would have been miserable, as inhabitants of the villages around Parícutin saw their fields buried under ash, or lava, and water sources dry up. Five months into the eruption, in July 1943, they were resettled to the newly built settlement of Caltzontzin, 20 kilometres distant, but out of reach of the ash. Here, people who had made their lives from farming at high altitudes on the plains had to adapt to living in a new location that had no connection to their original homes, and adapt their farming practices to lower elevations. Dionisio Pulido died in Caltzontzin in 1949; the volcanic eruption came to an end in 1952 and, in 1980, the main road to Caltzontzin was finally paved. Today, Parícutin is part of a national park and a tourist attraction, and what remains of the village of Parícutin is now entombed in rock.

## Laki, 1783

The eighteenth and nineteenth centuries saw three major volcanic eruptions whose legacies have helped to change the way that we think about volcanoes, and their consequences. The first of these was a dramatic eruption on the volcanic island of Iceland, an island that owes its very existence to plate tectonics and the 'oceanic ridge' on which it sits.

The summer of 1783 was marked across Europe for its strange weather. From late June through July 1783, observers noticed a persistent haze or dry fog, and summer temperatures reached the highest on record. In Worcestershire, a school teacher called William Dunn kept a weather diary (Figure 55). On 9 July he wrote:

> Wednesday Terrible Thunder and Lightning. 16 Sheep kill'd at Walton Hill a Farmer at Mansfield Park kill'd with his horse by lightning with a number of other beasts kill'd.
> …
> Thursday the Air continues in a Putrid state. The sun is red as blood with Thunder and Lightning with heavy rain.[69]

In the New Forest, William Gilpin, a vicar, writer and originator of the idea of the picturesque, also noticed something out of the ordinary. He was a prolific diarist and pasted newspaper clippings alongside his own commentaries and observations of the weather 'during twenty years from 1763 to 1785'. Gilpin's notes reveal how unusual the weather patterns were:

> What rendered it extraordinary was the state of the atmosphere. During almost all the summer months, the sky was overspread with a dark, dry fog. The vapours sometimes rolled about, as is usual in a dispersed storm: at other times, they clung like a heavy fog; and the sun, at noon day, appeared through them of that dark, dingy red, which it sometimes assumes through the haziness of a frosty evening.[70]

Figure 54 *previous page* View across the continental volcanic field of the Auvergne which is made up of multiple volcanic cones, many of which were formed in single eruptions. From George Poulett Scrope's *Memoir on the geology of central France*, 1827. Oxford, Bodleian Library, 2 DELTA 76, plate 4.

Figure 55 William Dunn's diary for July 1783, recording the 'putrid air' across England following the eruption of Laki. Oxford, Bodleian Library, MS. Don. c. 76, fols. 173v–174r.

This dry fog was reported from across continental Europe. Gilpin summarized the discussion about the origins of the haze:

> From what cause these dry fogs overspread the face of the earth was matter only of conjecture. Many were of the opinion that they were the affluvia of those dreadful earthquakes which had desolated Calabria [five large earthquakes had struck from February to March 1783]. No other sufficient cause could be ascribed, and that cause in its greatness at least appeared to be sufficient. … But the cause of these vapours was not easily found, their effects were undoubted. Never was remembered a year more remarkable for meteors, and thunderstorms; which indeed made it still more probable that these vapours originated from the sulphurous steams of earthquakes and volcanoes.[71]

That summer, tens of thousands of people across Europe suffered from breathing problems as a direct consequence of the poor air quality.

The hot summer was then followed by a very cold winter. Benjamin Franklin, at that time ambassador to Paris, also made the link to volcanic activity in Iceland as a possible cause, 'whether it was the vast quantity of smoke, long continuing, to issue during the summer from Hecla in Iceland, and that other volcano which arose out of the sea near that island, is yet uncertain'.[72]

On Iceland, there would have been no doubt about the origins of the dry fog. On 8 June 1783, violent steam and ash explosions began along a 50-kilometre-long fissure, near the central Icelandic volcano of Grimsvötn. Within four days, a full-scale fissure eruption of hot fluid basalt lava had begun, disgorging lava and volcanic gases at unprecedented rates. This was no short-lived eruption. By the time the Lakagigar or Laki eruption finally stopped, nine months later, 15 cubic kilometres of lava had been erupted – ten times larger than that at Parícutin and erupted in a tenth of the time. Volcanic ash and gases – a toxic mixture rich in carbon dioxide, sulphur dioxide and hydrogen fluoride – cast a grim pall across Iceland, poisoning water supplies and grazing lands. During violent episodes of eruption, the same gases were carried across the north Atlantic, where it arrived as a choking dry sulphurous fog. On Iceland, grazing animals died at an alarming rate, many from fluorosis. Within a year, a quarter of the Icelandic population had also died. The Laki eruption remains the largest and most damaging fissure eruption of historical times. In the space of just nine months, the volcano released as much sulphur dioxide into the atmosphere as all of the rest of the world's volcanoes typically release in a decade, creating what must be one of the world's worst natural pollution events.

## Tambora, 1815

The Laki eruption had dramatic environmental effects on the northern reaches of the globe, but the wider impacts of the eruption were limited since most of the ash and gas erupted remained low within the atmosphere. For volcanic eruptions to have a global impact, they need to inject ash and gases high enough into the atmosphere to ensure that the pollutants will spread around the globe. Typically, only eruption plumes that reach at least 20 kilometres in height, or twice the typical cruising height of a commercial aircraft, have this potential. This is the case in violently explosive 'Plinian' eruptions that form strongly convecting and buoyant plumes of ash and gas (Figure 56). Two catastrophic eruptions in Indonesia over the past 250 years stand out for their size and effects – Tambora and Krakatoa.

The great eruption of Tambora, on Sumbawa Island, in April 1815 was the largest known explosive eruption of the past 500 years, and caused the worst known volcanic loss of life. Global perturbations from Tambora left a clear environmental fingerprint, and there are stories from around the world of unusual weather, crop failures and famine during the 'year without a summer' of 1816.

Much of what we know about the eruption is down to the efforts of Stamford Raffles, a British colonial official, and Heinrich Zollinger, a Swiss zoologist. In 1815, Thomas Stamford Raffles was temporary governor of Java, which the British had invaded four years earlier. After Tambora erupted, he sent Lieutenant Owen Phillips to deliver supplies of rice for relief and to collect eyewitness accounts of the eruption.

Before the eruption Tambora was a classically cone-shaped volcanic peak of considerable stature and visible for many kilometres around. The footprint of the volcano forms the Sanggar peninsula, on the island of Sumbawa. It is likely that the volcano had been rumbling for some years, but activity didn't begin in earnest until 1 April 1815. A letter to Raffles from a resident of Banyuwangi, Java, 400 kilometres west of the Sanggar peninsula, describes this stage of the activity:

> At ten PM of the first of April we heard a noise resembling a cannonade, which lasted at intervals till nine o'clock next day; it continued at times loud, at others resembling distant thunder; but on the night of the 10th, the explosions became truly tremendous. On the morning of the 3rd April, ashes began to fall like fine snow; and in the course of the day they were half-an-inch deep on the ground. From that time till the 11th the air was continuously impregnated with them to such a degree that it was unpleasant to stir out of doors. On the morning of the 11th, the opposite shore of Bali was completely obscured in a dense cloud, which gradually approached the Java shore and was dreary and terrific.[73]

The eruption reached a climax on 10–11 April, as vividly described by the Rajah of Sanggar:

> About seven PM on the 10th of April, three distinct columns of flame burst forth near the top of Tomboro mountain … and after ascending separately to a very great height, their caps united in the air. In a short time the whole mountain next Sangar appeared like a body of liquid fire extending itself in every direction.[74]

Figure 56 Sketch of an eruption plume from Krakatoa in May 1883, three months before the climatic phase of the eruption. Drawn from a photograph. Royal Society Krakatoa Committee, Symons *et al.*, *The eruption of Krakatoa and subsequent phenomena*, Trübner, London, 1888. Oxford, Bodleian Library, Vet. A7 c.45.

This captures the moment that hot, dense clouds of pumice and ash – pyroclastic flows – rushed down the sides of the volcano, engulfing and burying villages in their path. At about this same time, the final collapse and destruction of the volcanic cone began, leaving a great crater or caldera in the decapitated mountaintop. The pyroclastic flows caused great loss of life, travelling as they do at speeds that are faster than people can run, and causing death with a combination of searing heat and dense choking ash. Similar phenomena – pyroclastic flows, *nuées ardentes*, or 'burning clouds' – have been

responsible for many of the worst volcanic calamities known, from the burial of Pompeii in 79 CE, to the destruction of the city of St Pierre, Martinique, in May 1902.

The geological deposits left behind by these flows are quite distinctive and can be recognized in many volcanic areas of the world – testaments to great eruptions of the past. In some parts of the world – Kyushu, Japan; the central Andes of Chile and Bolivia; the ancient volcanic plateaux of Colorado to name just a few – they form vast sheets of pumice, rock and ash, in places welded to a dense glassy rock with vivid colours from white to yellow and orange, red or black. The deposits of some of these eruptions are of a staggering scale: tens to hundreds of metres thick, forming landscape-covering sheets that extend for tens to hundreds of kilometres from the original volcanic source. The largest of these record eruptions are of an almost unimaginable scale – eruptions of thousands of cubic kilometres of magma, erupted in a geological instant, and many times larger than anything seen in the past 2,000 years of human history.

Heinrich Zollinger was a Swiss botanist, who moved to Java in 1841. In 1847, he led an expedition to see what remained of Tambora. He was the first scientist to climb to the crater rim since the 1815 eruption, and the first to document the severe local impacts of the eruption. Zollinger estimated that on Sumbawa alone 10,100 people were killed in the eruption. Another 48,000 died later of hunger or illness across Sumbawa and Lombok islands.

In Europe, the eruption had passed essentially unnoticed. This was well before the invention of the telegraph, and news travelled only as fast as the ships that brought the letters. It was also the culmination of Napoleon Bonaparte's Hundred Days campaign, in between escaping imprisonment on the isle of Elba, facing defeat at the Battle of Waterloo and eventually being exiled to one of the most remote volcanic islands in the world, St Helena.

In *The Times* on 21 November 1815 a letter from Java mentioned the 'most tremendous eruptions of the mountain Tomboro, that ever perhaps took place in any part of the world'. However, it wasn't until the summer of 1816 that the wider effects of the eruption began to be felt around the globe. *The Times* of 20 July 1816 noted:

> The continuance of the present very unseasonable weather. Such an
> inclement summer is scarcely remembered by the oldest inhabitant

Figure 57 Sampson White's weather diary for July 1816, from the 'year without a summer' that followed the 1815 eruption of Tambora. Saturday 27 July: 'No rain!!'. Oxford, Bodleian Library, MS. Eng. misc. c. 198, fol. 125r.

| | | | Bar | Ther | Wind |
|---|---|---|---|---|---|
| | | **Sunday 21st July.** | | | |
| | | Heavy Showers. | | | |
| 59 | | SW served Mandford Adolou McKinley | 29 | 64 | S |
| | | FHW afternoon Prayers and dined | 2/10 | | |
| | | TW saw pd 20 an aunt | | | |
| | | **Monday 22nd Showery.** | | | |
| | | Tom and Maria dined at Blakely | 29 | | |
| 63 | | Wine from Mr Hilyards, Northston | 1/10 | 64 | SW |
| | | port eleven Bottles at | | | |
| | | Cape Madeira. thirteen Bottles at | | | |
| | | John weeding. | | | |
| | | **Tuesday 23rd Showery** | | | |
| | | Glyd came and dined. Do FHW. | | | |
| 62 | | Mare from Blakely the first and | 29 | 63 | SW |
| | | Do Cucumber !! | 2/10 | | |
| | | John odd Jobs. | | | |
| | | **Wednesday 24th Heavy Showers.** | | | |
| | | Glyd called and went home. | | | |
| 63 | | Glyd budded two Bullace Stocks planted | 29 | 65 | S |
| | | on SW side of House with apricots | 2/10 | | |
| | | Note fr: Mr Hodgson. | | | |
| | | John weeding. Thunder heard remote | | | |
| | | **Thursday 25th Heavy Showers.** | | | |
| 62 | | Raked over some of the Hay in | 29 | 66 | SW |
| | | Home close - spoiled by the Wet. | 3/10 | | |
| | | John absent. | | | var |
| | | **Friday 26th Showery. Rain Bow vesp.** | | | |
| 66 | | Set out more annuals. | 29 | 65 | W |
| | | | 4/10 | | var |
| | | John weeding. | | | |
| | | **Saturday 27th No rain !! the first** | | | |
| | | dry Day for 24 Days. | | | |
| 66 | | Turned the remainder of the Hay in | 29 | 64 | W |
| | | close | 3/10 | | |
| | | John odd jobs pd John in full | | | |

of London. The hay towards the southern counties has so much been injured by the incessant rains that the only alternative … is to convert it into dung for manure. Should the present wet weather continue, the corn will inevitably be laid, and the effects cannot be other than ruinous to the farmers.[75]

In the village of Maidford, Northamptonshire, Hannah White was keeping a weather log-book for her husband, the Revd Samson White, 'because he is too lazy to keep it himself!'[76] Her entry for 27 July (Figure 57) reads: 'No rain!! The first dry day for 24 days.'[77]

In Quebec, Canada, there was heavy snow in June, 'a state of weather entirely unexampled in the memory of the inhabitants', while in Norfolk, Virginia, a correspondent wrote in May 1816 that 'the weather is uncommonly cold. To what cause it may be ascribed we do not say, but we do believe the general coldness or backwardness of spring has never been experienced in the same degree as the present'.

Wider consequences of the dismal summer included crop failures and famine across parts of Europe, Asia and the eastern United States. In Switzerland, some people were so hungry they ate cat flesh to survive. In the summer of 1816, Lord Byron, Percy Bysshe Shelley and Mary Wollstonecraft Godwin took a holiday on the shores of Lake Geneva. Bad weather, caused by the aftermath of the eruption, kept them indoors and to pass the time they invented ghost stories. Here, Mary came up with the idea for the novel *Frankenstein* (Figure 58).

Further north, shifting weather patterns began to open up the fabled 'Northwest Passage', a sea route that offered the promise of linking the Atlantic and Pacific oceans through the straits between western Greenland and Canada. John Barrow, a British naval administrator, commissioned expeditions by John Ross and William Parry in 1818 and 1819 that made great progress. Unfortunately, these were also the last years for which the effects of the Tambora eruption can be seen in the temperature records, and later expeditions by Parry in 1821 and 1824, and John and James Clark Ross in 1829 failed to make the anticipated breakthrough, as the climate system returned to its former state.

Geological studies have helped to piece together the story of why the eruption had such a significant impact on global weather patterns. The eruption ejected about 100

Figure 58 Mary Shelley's *Frankenstein*, draft of the opening of vol. I chapter 7. Mary Shelley came up with the idea for the novel in the terrible summer of 1816 while on holiday at Lake Geneva. Oxford, Bodleian Library, MS. Abinger c. 56, fol. 21r.

It was on a dreary night of November
that I beheld ~~the frame on which~~ my man compleated, ~~and~~
with an anxiety that almost amount
ed to agony I collected instruments of life
around me and ~~endeavoured~~ that I might infuse a
spark of being into the lifeless thing
that lay at my feet. It was already
one in the morning, the rain pattered
dismally against the window panes &
my candle was nearly burnt out, when
by the glimmer of the half extinguish
ed light I saw the dull yellow eye of
the creature open — It breathed hard,
and a convulsive motion agitated
its limbs.

But ~~how~~ How can I describe my
emotion at this catastrophe, or how deli
neate the wretch whom with such
infinite pains and care I had endeavoured
to form. His limbs were in proportion
and I had selected his features & as
beautiful. ~~handsome~~ ~~handsome~~ Beautiful; Great God! His
yellow ~~dun~~ skin scarcely covered the work of
muscles and arteries beneath; his hair
was flowing and his teeth of a pearly white
ness but these luxuriances only ~~formed~~
formed a more horrid contrast with
his watery eyes that seemed almost of
the same colour as the dun white
sockets in which they were set,

of a lustrous black &

cubic kilometres of volcanic ash and about 60 million tonnes of sulphur dioxide high into the atmosphere – perhaps as high as 35 kilometres. The volcanic sulphur slowly reacted to form tiny droplets of sulphate that spread like a veil around the globe. This high-altitude haze scattered sunlight for the next two to three years, causing a temporary global cooling. In terms of volcano-metrics, Tambora was about six times larger than the last major eruption on Earth, the 1991 eruption of Mount Pinatubo, Philippines; it rates as a seven on the volcanic explosivity index.

Two hundred years on from Tambora, it is worthwhile reflecting on the challenges that a future eruption of this scale would pose, whether it were to occur in Indonesia or elsewhere. Our ability to measure volcanic restlessness should help us to spot that something is amiss before the start of an eruption; but would we be able to identify the possible size of the eruption, or its impact, in advance? Probably not, and we need to do much more to prepare for and mitigate the local, regional and global consequences of a repeat of an eruption of this scale. But one thing that we can do is to make sure that we have learnt all that we can from the past.

## Krakatoa, 1883

The great eruption of Krakatoa (or Krakatau) in Indonesia in August 1883 has become the archetype of a volcanic catastrophe. Unlike Tambora, this eruption made the headlines around the world, in part because newly installed undersea cables allowed the news of the event to be wired rapidly across the globe. The Krakatoa eruption was one of the first major eruptions to be intensively studied by scientists. The journal *Nature* published an editorial on the 'Java Catastrophe' shortly after news of the eruption broke. By this stage it was already clear that 'the most potent agent of destruction … would seem to have been the great sea-wave' triggered during the eruption, and that there had been 'great changes in the form and outlines of the volcanic island of Krakatoa'.[78]

Over the next few weeks, numerous reports gave descriptions and explanations of some of the many widespread effects of the eruption – from the appearance of great floating rafts of pumice to the pressure-waves, earthquakes and remarkable sunsets that accompanied the event. In February 1884, the Royal Society set up the Krakatoa Committee, chaired by a meteorologist, George Symons, to collect information on

Figure 59  Chart of the Sunda Straits, Indonesia, in 1794. Krakatoa was at this stage a dormant volcano on Cracatoa or Crocatore Island, which is noted as a 'very convenient waiting place' for ships to collect water and provisions. *A new chart of the straits of Sunda, 1794*. Oxford, Bodleian Library, (E) D40:(6).

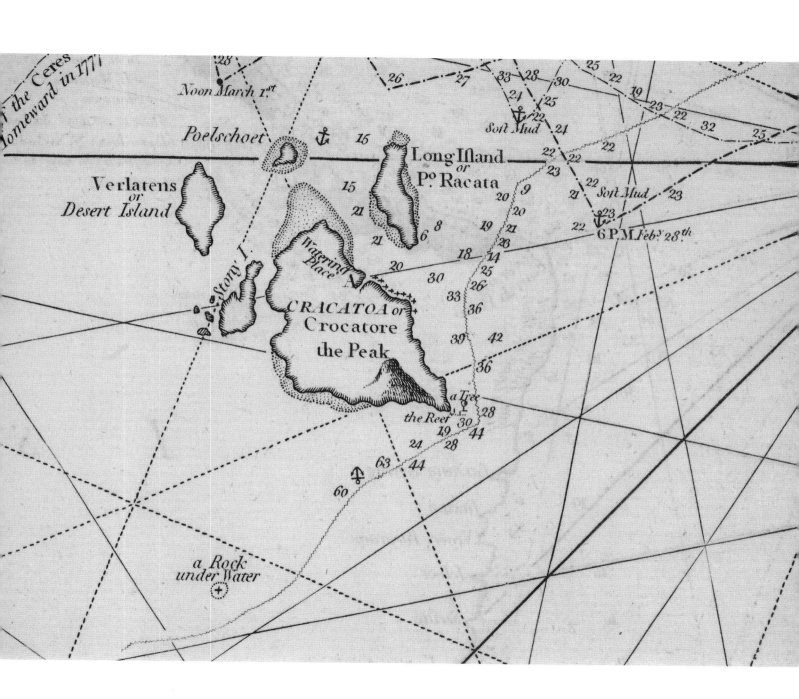

# Twilight and Afterglow effects at Chelsea, London, Nov. 26th 1883.

Nº1. About 4·10 P.M.

Nº2. About 4·20 P.M.

W. Ashcroft. Del.

Lith. & Imp. Camb. Sci. Inst. Co.

Nº3. About 4·30 P.M.

Nº 4. About 4·40 P.M.

Nº 5. About 5 P.M.

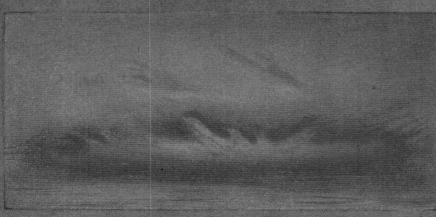

W. ASCROFT. DEL.

LITH. & IMP. CAMB. SCI. INST. Cº.

Nº 6. About 5·15 P.M.

'the various accounts of the volcanic eruption … and its attendant phenomena', including 'authenticated facts respecting the fall of pumice and dust … unusual disturbances of barometric pressure and sea level … and exceptional effects of light and colour in the atmosphere'.[79] These results were published in 1888 in a wonderful monograph, which is still one of the most complete accounts of a major volcanic eruption and its widespread effects. The most celebrated scientific impact of the Krakatoa eruption was the recognition that the spectacular sunsets that followed the eruption must be the consequences of the global spread of volcanic pollutants, high in the atmosphere (Figure 60).

Although the Krakatoa eruption (Figure 61) was one of the largest eruptions of the past 200 years, it is not exceptional compared with eruptions from the geological record. It rates as a six on the volcanic explosivity index, and eruptions of this size occur once every century or so, somewhere around the globe. Krakatoa remains the best-documented example of a 'caldera-forming' eruption, during which the entire edifice of the volcano collapses. The eruption had catastrophic consequences for tens of thousands of people living along the shores of Java and Sumatra, since the huge displacements of seawater during the eruption and the collapse of the volcano triggered major tsunamis that swept ashore, causing great destruction.

Krakatoa began to grow again after only a very short hiatus. By 1927, a new island, Anak Krakatoa, had grown up from the seabed and begun to emerge above the surf. In February 1931, British naturalist William Bristowe set off with a Russian and a Hungarian 'who was stone deaf from a volcanic bang in Java' (a damaging eruption of Merapi that had killed 1,400 people). Since Krakatoa had first reappeared with jets of steam and debris, it had risen and vanished again four times. Bristowe hoped to set foot on Anak Krakatoa V, which reappeared in August 1931.

> A first glimpse came as we were passing the white pumice cliffs of Krakatoa, and the stern grey crater of Rakata where Krakatoa had been split in half
>
> …
>
> A feeling of disappointment was uppermost at seeing what looked like a flat toasted biscuit floating on the sea, nearly ¾ of a mile in length, but only 30 feet above sea level.[80]
>
> …
>
> There, with feelings of intense jubilation, I leaped on to its virgin shore composed entirely of dark grey ash, black cinders and white pumice stone. The only abundant insects were scavengers which could feed on whatever plant life the sea brought them – springtails, beetles. Ants, moths and a mosquito were probably stray arrivals. At that date, the south western fringe of the crater was heated by quantities of gas bubbles coming up from below sea level; we drew back before long because of the hot ground under our feet.[81]

Before the end of 1932, fungi, algae and bacteria had all been found in the new soil of the island, and shore plants had begun to grow. A new crater emerged in an eruption in 1933, and the island has continued to grow ever since.

Figure 60 *previous page* William Ascroft's watercolours of vivid sunsets seen from Chelsea, London, in autumn 1883 after the great eruption of Krakatoa. From Symons et al., *The eruption of Krakatoa and subsequent phenomena*, Trübner, London, 1888. Oxford, Bodleian Library, Vet. A7 c.45.

Figure 61 Image of Krakatoa after its reawakening in the 1930s. Private collection

# CHAPTER 6
## Living with volcanoes

WHAT IS IT LIKE living next to a volcano? Today, more than 500 million people live near volcanoes, and many communities have long coexisted with the volcano in their back yard (Figure 62). Over the past 100 years and more, volcanologists have become better and better at measuring and monitoring volcanoes, in the hope that they will be better able to spot the build-up to the next eruption before it happens. But although we now have a whole armoury of instruments on, under and above the ground that we can deploy in volcanic emergencies, many of the most significant volcanic eruptions of the past century have occurred at volcanoes that had been inactive for many hundreds of years. Equally, many of the worst volcanic disasters have occurred either where the sudden onset of activity and then eruption took people by surprise or where the activity escalated in ways that people near the volcano were not prepared for. With some notable exceptions – such as the two Mexican volcanoes of Jorullo and Parícutin, that grew from nowhere in spectacular eruptions in 1759 and 1948 – we mostly know where volcanoes are, and most eruptions happen somewhere near or around the summit, or the main crater or vent. Reconstructing past volcanic eruptions and their consequences, and learning from the experiences of people who have lived with volcanoes in their back yard, can help us to learn valuable lessons about how best to reduce the effects of future volcanic disasters.

## Montserrat

Montserrat, the 'Emerald isle' of the Caribbean, is a small mountainous island near Antigua, towards the northern, or leeward, end of the Lesser Antilles volcanic arc. Before 1995, this green teardrop of an island showed only gentle signs of its volcanic

Figure 62  Farmers living on the flanks of Gede volcano, Java, Indonesia. A lava flow partly fills the landslide scar formed during a past eruption, and the summit crater steams. Gede was frequently active during the nineteenth century and last erupted in 1957. Johannes Muller, *Beschreibung der Insel Java*, 1860. Oxford, Bodleian Library, (OC) 246 h.70.

heritage. Some clusters of small earthquakes struck in the late 1800s, the 1930s and again in the 1960s. Nestling around the rugged hills in the south of the island were some steaming sulphurous fumaroles and hot springs, known as Soufrières. Amerindians settled the island at least 2,000 years ago, and by the time that the first Europeans arrived, Montserrat was home to the Caribs, who knew the island as Alliouagana. There were no records of any volcanic activity since the early 1600s.

On 18 July 1995, the volcano sputtered suddenly back to life, with the 'roar of a jet engine'.[82] Steam and ash began to paint a pall of grey within English's crater and around the summit of the rejuvenated Soufrière Hills volcano. Montserrat moved to high alert, as the people began to come to terms with what was happening, and scientists set about building the monitoring infrastructure needed to watch an active volcano. On 21 August, a large explosion sent a cold, wet blanket of ash that slowly descended across the main town of Plymouth, plunging the town into darkness. Over the next two days, 6,000 people – more than half of the population of the island – fled to find temporary shelter, and the cycle of alerts and evacuations began.

This, as we now know, was just the beginning of an extended eruption, in which pulses of activity would be interspersed with extended 'pauses' – periods when the volcano was quieter, but not yet dormant. For three years, the volcanic crisis worsened. It reached a nadir on 25 June 1997, when pyroclastic currents swept north and east from the volcano. Hot ash clouds reached the airport and inundated valleys, fields and villages in their path, killing 19 people. This was a shocking moment in the eruption, later captured in verse by Montserrat poet and historian Howard Fergus: '[An] inauspicious day in June, when birth / and death walked hand in hand, on farms / at Farms and Farrells garnering rhizomes / from shallow graves among the furrows.'[83] By the end of 1997, the island was at its most stretched. Two-thirds of the island was out of bounds and 7,000 people had left. Plymouth, the capital, had been permanently evacuated two years earlier and many thriving communities were now ash-coated ghost towns (Figure 63). Of those who remained, more were living in shelters – churches, schools, tin huts and wooden chalets.

My first visit to Montserrat was in early 1998, following the then well-trodden path to join the Montserrat Volcano Observatory. The Mongo Hill observatory was a house in the north of the island, with no line of sight to the volcano, which was about to enter

Figure 63 The centre of Plymouth, the former capital of Montserrat, in 1998. The telephone booth and clock tower are buried under mud and blocks washed from the volcano. © David M. Pyle.

its first pause. For the first week of February 1998, the volcano coughed ash. Every eight hours there were pulses of earthquakes as avalanches of rock fell from the dome. None of these earthquakes was large enough to be felt, but during each pulse of activity vast orange–grey clouds of dust or ash rose from the volcano. These clouds drifted across the island, sprinkling everything with gritty powder. As the clumps of ash landed they broke up into tiny dust particles which formed an irritating, choking haze, coating everything with a stubborn grey film. In the space of two days, 50,000 tonnes of ash smothered the island under a layer of what looked like cement.

In September 2012, I returned, this time with colleagues who were running a workshop looking back at people's experiences of the eruption. A lot had changed on Montserrat in the intervening years. The eruption had continued in pulses and pauses, and settled into a pattern of behaviour that is both familiar and that can be lived with. Plymouth remained abandoned and out of bounds (Figure 64), but outside the immediate perimeter of the volcano and the debris-strewn fans that tumbled down its sides, much of the landscape had recovered. Communities that had once been inside the exclusion zone had now been open again for a decade, and a purpose-built volcano observatory now occupies a prominent viewpoint overlooking the steaming volcano. The island was again green and vibrant, with gardens splashed with the rich reds of bougainvillea and hibiscus.

There are ambitious plans for the future, building new capacity for tourists and other activities in the north of the island, which has only occasionally been directly affected by the volcanic activity. The strongest evidence for the strength of resolve of the residents of Montserrat, and of the bright signs for the future, came from the workshop and the stories of those who had lived through the darkest days of the eruption. Speaker after speaker captivated the audience with their personal journeys of survival and resilience. One common theme was the role played by poetry and song in coping with the stress, hardship and loss experienced by communities across the island. Herman 'Cupid' Francis was a teacher before the eruption, and now four-time Calypso Monarch and Montserrat's Director of Culture. He captured the spirit of 1996, the height of the crisis when people were being displaced from their homes and livelihoods, with his song 'when you go don't go too far … take the road that leads you home'.[84]

The eruption of Montserrat exemplifies many of the particular challenges of living on a small island when a long-dormant volcano returns to life. In 1995 there were no cultural or other memories of what it was like to live through an eruption. And the people, their communities and the state had no preparations or plans in hand to deal with what was about to unfold.

## St Vincent

Four hundred kilometres south of Montserrat, St Vincent is a rugged tropical island in the southern Caribbean seas. You might recognize it as the backdrop to *Pirates of the Caribbean*. The active volcano on St Vincent is also a Soufrière, a name shared by many other volcanic sites in the Antilles. While the geological record of past eruptions of St Vincent stretches back for hundreds of thousands of years, the historical record of

Figure 64  Office supplies, abandoned since Plymouth was evacuated in 1996. © David M. Pyle.

known eruptions is short. The first documented eruption of St Vincent was in March 1718. At this time, the island was inhabited by Caribs, and had not yet been colonized by the French or British. There was a lot of trade across the region, and many passing ships to report on the events. On 5 July 1718, an anonymous pamphlet was published in London describing 'the destruction of the isle of St Vincent'. This account was compiled from sailors' accounts, and later discovered to have been written by Daniel Defoe, who went on to publish *Robinson Crusoe* a year later.

On 22 March 1718, a French ship passed by St Vincent, and stopped to buy fish from the inhabitants, who came out in three canoes. The locals reported they had been terribly frightened by earthquakes for some time, had seen flashes of fire like lightning which did not come from the clouds as usual but out of the earth. Four days later, late at night, the eruption started with a bang:

> Ships both at sea, and in ports in several islands reported that they saw in the night that terrible flash of fire, and after that they heard innumerable clashes of thunder – some say it was thunder they heard, others that it was cannon – only that the noise was a thousand times as loud as thunder or cannon.
>
> The next morning, when the day began to break, the air looked dismally. All overhead was a deep impenetrable darkness; but below, all round the edge of the horizon, it looked as if the heavens were all on fire. As the day came on, still the darkness increased, till it was far darker than it had been in any part of the night before and, as they thought, the cloud descended upon them. The darkness still increased after this, and in the afternoon they were surprised with the falling of something upon them as thick as smoke, but fine as dust, and yet as solid as sand; this fell thicker and faster as they were nearer or farther off – some ships had it nine inches, others a foot thick on their deck; the island of Martinique is covered with it at about seven to nine inches thick; at Barbados it is frightful, even to St Christopher's it exceeded four inches.[85]

Figure 65   The summit crater of the Soufrière of St Vincent in 1784. *Philosophical Transactions of the Royal Society of London*, vol. 75, 1785, pp. 16–31. © The Royal Society.

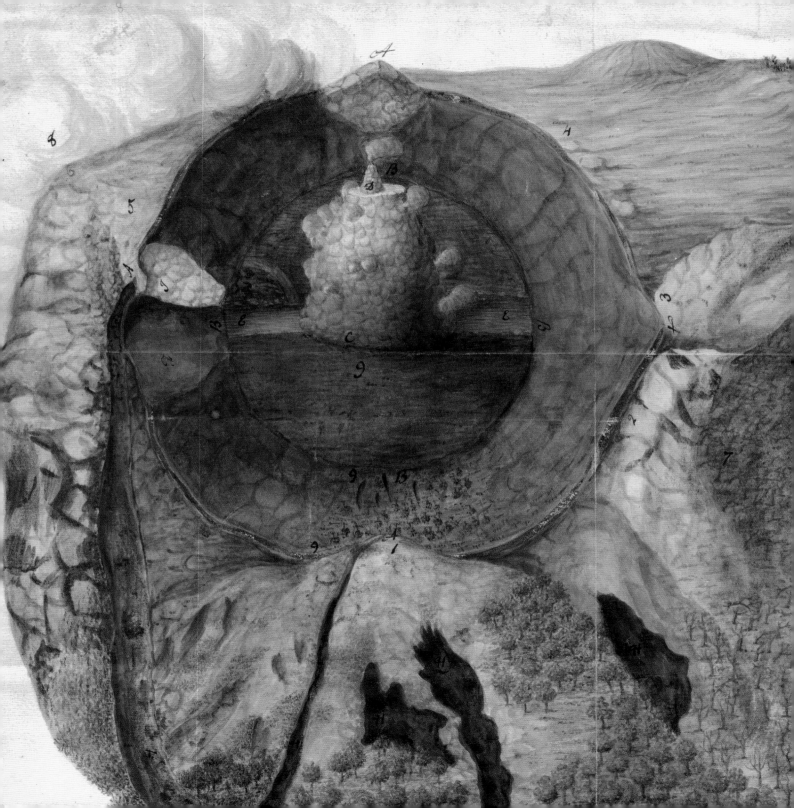

Ash fell for another two or three days across Barbados, before the activity died down. Defoe recognized that whatever had happened was similar to the activity of volcanoes with which he was familiar, such as Etna in Sicily, Vesuvius near Naples and Hekla, Iceland. Nothing more is known of the eruption, or its consequences.

Over the next seventy years, the islands of the Caribbean were fought over and colonized by the British, French and Dutch. The British took over St Vincent in 1763, and set about surveying the island and carving up the best lands for cultivation. In 1765, Robert Melville, Governor in Chief of the Windward Isles, established a botanical research station to develop and grow new economic crops. The Botanic Gardens were soon growing cinnamon, nutmeg and mango trees, and winning awards for the promotion of agriculture. Breadfruit from Tahiti was eventually introduced to the island by Captain Bligh in 1793, after his first attempt had ended in mutiny.

A Scottish botanist, Alexander Anderson, climbed to the crater of the Soufrière in 1784. His report of the 'mountain of Morne Garou and the volcano in its summit' included a view of the summit crater,[86] partly filled with water and with a steaming lava dome at its centre (Figure 65), a view remarkably similar to the present day. Anderson later took over as superintendent of the Botanic Gardens.

Nothing is known of any activity at the volcano until 1812. By then St Vincent was a major exporter of sugar to European markets. Most of the 26,000 inhabitants of the island were slaves working on the plantations in grim conditions. The few communities of indigenous Caribs had been excluded from the best lands and lived mainly in the northern and north-eastern parts of the island. After several months of tremors and rumblings, a major explosive eruption began on 27 April. Hugh Perry Keane, a barrister and plantation owner, recorded the unfolding events in his diaries:

> Weds 29 [April] Then to see the Souffrier, involved in dark clouds and vomiting black sands. Landed at Wallilabou. Spent the evening in contemplation of the volcano, and slept there.
> [Thurs 30th]. In the afternoon the rousing of the Mountain increased and at 7 o'clock the flames burst forth and the dreadful eruption began. All night watching it between 2 & 5 o'clock in the morning showers of

stones & earthquakes threatened our immediate destruction.
[May 1]. The day did not give light till nearly 9 – the whole island involved in gloom. The mountain was quiet all night.
Sun 3rd Rose at 7 and after gathering some Bfast ... Proceeded to Wallibu – strange and dismal sight, the river dried up and the land covered with cinders and sulphur. Morne Ronde Hid in smoke and ashes – the track covered with trees & a new formation given to it – burnt carcasses of cattle lying everywhere.[87]

News of the 1812 eruption travelled quickly back to London, where it featured as a leading article in late June – quite likely written by Keane. 'The birth of May dawned like the day of judgement. A chaotic gloom enveloped the mountain, and an impenetrable haze hung over the sea with black sluggish clouds of a sulphurous cast; the whole island was covered with ... cinders, scoria and broken masses of volcanic matter.'[88] Keane's pencil sketch of the eruption was later used by the painter Joseph Turner to create a dramatic image of the eruption of the Souffrier Mountains, in the Island of St Vincent, at midnight on 30 April 1812 (Figure 66).

The eruption had severe consequences for people and properties in the northern reaches of the island. Estates on both the leeward and windward sides of the island were affected by torrents of wet ash; two of the largest rivers in the north of the island (Wallibou and Rabacca) dried up; and 'yet, strange to tell, very few lives have been lost'. In total, 56 people are thought to have died in the eruption or its immediate aftermath.

Plantation owners petitioned the British government for compensation explaining that parts of the island 'have suffered in an extreme degree; the showers of volcanic matter ... having covered the whole surface of the ground about ten inches deep', and that this was an Act of God for which they should not bear the penalty: 'Your Lordship's Memorialists would humbly represent, that the present case is not only novel in its nature, but unexampled in any of His Majesty's dominions for much more than a century. It is a contingency that could not have been contemplated when the lands were purchased from the Crown four years ago at prices far exceeding any of the lands in His Majesty's Colonies in the West Indies.'[89]

Figure 66 The explosive eruption of the Soufrière of St Vincent in 1812, painted by J.M.W. Turner, from a sketch by Hugh Perry Keane. University of Liverpool Art Gallery & Collections, UK / Bridgeman Images.

The appeal was successful, setting both an extraordinary precedent and ensuring that the sugar estates in the north of St Vincent that had just been destroyed in the eruption would be rebuilt, in the same place.

Ninety years passed before the volcano reawakened. In this time slavery had been abolished, the bottom had fallen out of the sugar market and two damaging hurricanes had laid waste to the island. The second of these, in September 1898, wreaked havoc, destroying the housing of more than half the population, damaging many of the plantation estates buildings and killing hundreds. In the preceding five years, the value of sugar exports had fallen by more than 60 per cent and the industry was in terminal decline. Absentee landlords, who still owned most of the land, were leaving their estates abandoned and unproductive, and islanders were caught in desperate poverty, with no work and no land on which to subsist. A Royal Commission proposed a radical programme of land reform, which was just about to start when a new eruption struck.

## May 1902

After ninety years of quiescence, the summit of the volcano would have been a tranquil spot, with a deep lake filling the old crater. In February and March 1901, earthquakes were felt in parts of the north of the island. By April 1902, tremors had increased in number and strength, triggering landslides and rock falls near the summit of the mountain. Concern grew about the possibility of an eruption, partly because of the memories of 1812, and also because there were reports of intensifying volcanic activity at Mont Pelée on nearby Martinique.

It was a clear day on 6 May 1902 and the whole lip of the crater could be seen from the south-west side. There had been overnight reports of clouds of steam and a bright glow from the volcano summit. Rumbling sounds like thunder were heard through the morning and there were some distinct shocks of earthquakes. Some residents living on the flanks of the volcano had begun to leave their homes. A group of women walked past the crater on their way to sell fish in Georgetown, reaching the summit in late morning. They reported feeling the hill shaking and smelling strongly of sulphur. The lake had changed colour, no longer blue-green but milky-white to red in places, boiling and steaming. Through the afternoon, activity intensified, with great columns of steam and sharp detonations. At the foot of the volcano, in the west of the island, people were in no doubt that an eruption was beginning, and large numbers of people began to evacuate.

Estate owner T. M. McDonald landed on the beach near the Richmond Vale estate at 6 pm: 'The summit of the Soufriere was enveloped in the usual white cloud, and at first nothing unusual was visible. Within a minute or two of landing, someone exclaimed "Soufriere bursting now" and could see enormous vertical columns of white vapour being ejected, virtually noiselessly, and was now quite convinced that an eruption had been and was now taking place.'[90]

By the morning of Wednesday 7 May 1902, the activity of the Soufrière of St Vincent had picked up significantly in intensity. Close to the volcano, witnesses reported strong outbursts, clouds of steam and, by around 11 am, thunder, lightning and showers of black material being thrown outwards from the column of vapour. In the town of Chateaubelair, south-east of the volcano, a continuous stream of evacuees was arriving, and by 1 pm, pebbles and ashes had begun to fall:

> A little before 2 o'clock vast spiral clouds of thick greyish white smoke in fleecy rolls, began to rise high in the heavens, visible from across the whole island, and streaked with intensely vivid pencil flashes of lightning. A pall of smoke spread itself ever more widely over the heavens. At 2.40 scoriae, approximately the size of pence and half-pence, began to fall thickly in Kingstown accompanied by a steady rain of volcanic dust, which last has continued to the present time, though much lighter now than at first. The sulphurous odour of this dust is very strong. By 4 o'clock the sky was completely blotted out by a murky pall of yellow vapour the conditions approximating to those attending the less noxious variety of yellow London fog.[91]

The eruption peaked that afternoon. McDonald recorded what he saw from the water: 'Left Richmond Vale House. Saw vapour as we rowed hard across Chateaubelair Bay coming down to sea level. Sea peppered all around with stones. A terrific huge red and purplish curtain advancing after the racing boat.'

Passengers on another rowing boat had to jump out to escape the searing heat of the descending ash cloud. Their testimonies were recounted in Anderson and Flett's accounts of the eruption, published in the *Philosophical Transactions of the Royal Society*: 'In a moment it was pitch black and intensely hot and stifling. They threw themselves into the sea to escape burning by the hot sand. They all dived, and when they returned to the surface the air was still unfit to breathe and the heat intense. So they continued to dive repeatedly.'[92] During this climactic phase of the eruption, thick dense and hot pyroclastic avalanches raced down the steep slopes of the Soufrière, stripping vegetation and leaving a trail of thick deposits as they went. Hot wet flows of ash and debris cascaded down the river valleys, perhaps fed by boiling waters from the crater (Figure 67). Few people caught up in this calamity would have survived.

News of the unfolding emergency began to reach the outside world, but there were difficulties as the volcanic activity had caused slumping on the sea floor, cutting the submarine telegraph cables.

Robert Llewelyn, Governor of the Windward Islands, telegraphed the Colonial Office in London: '7 May. Confirm eruption of Soufrière. Four outbursts since 3 pm yesterday; inhabitants much alarmed in the surrounding country are swarming into Chateaubelair; 300 fed last night. Disturbance not felt Kingstown.'[93] In his update on 11 May [From St Lucia]: 'By latest reports Saint Vincent damage confined to the north of the Island. Deaths estimated at five hundred.'[94]

From the Colonial office in London, Joseph Chamberlain authorized Llewelyn 'to draw upon the Crown agents for £1000 at once, and, if necessary, for more'. He added: 'Report carefully … after full consideration probable needs and expenditure. If amongst the killed or injured any prominent residents with relatives in this country telegraph names.'[95]

In reply, Llewelyn gave a quick update:

> Country on East coast … apparently struck and devastated similarly to St Pierre, and I fear that practically all living things within that radius have been killed, probably 1600; exact number never will be known; managers and overseers of estates with their families and several better class people killed. One thousand bodies found and buried, 160 sent

Figure 67 The ash-coated slopes of the once-vegetated Soufrière of St Vincent, following the explosive eruption of May 1902. Photograph by Tempest Anderson, 1904. © York Museums Trust.

Lot 14. Devastated Plantation.
Geol. Jn'l. Pl. X.                    D.a.190

into hospital in Georgetown; details too harrowing to describe. I have got the coasting steamer from St Lucia running up and down Leeward coast with water and provisions. I have asked Governor, Trinidad, to lend me medical officers and ordered one from Grenada. All neighbouring British Colonies giving assistance generously. The awful calamity is now realised, and every effort is being made to grapple with it. All the best sugar estates in the Carib country are devastated and the cattle dead. All officers and residents co-operating with me, and ladies making articles of clothing.[96]

The effects of the eruption on the north of the island were devastating (Figures 68 and 69). Of the 4,000 people who had been living there, 1,600 were dead and many others injured: hundreds suffering from burns; and others from fractures caused by falling debris. Llewelyn drew up a map of the area, which, he reported, was

> *devastated completely* by which I mean entirely covered with dust, ashes lava etc on which every tree is killed all herbage buried … It is a sad picture the best sugar estates, and the most fertile part of the island now turned into a heap of ashes, with not a living creature on it. The general loss on the island outside the devastated area is considerable as dust and ashes fell in varying quantities everywhere so that ground products and grass for fodder have suffered to a considerable extent causing the death of animals or the necessity of shipping them at great loss to the owners. Breadfruit and other fruits, even in Kingstown, are dropping from the trees as if blighted.[97]

The response to the eruption was quick, but muddled. Ships arrived from the United States and Barbados carrying so much rice that it had eventually to be sold off to stop it going mouldy. At the peak of the crisis, 7,000 people needed relief and were living on daily rations of food. The land reform process had just begun, so rapid progress was made in building new houses to resettle the displaced. The botanical station and agricultural school were quick to distribute new plants for the smallholders to become

Figure 68 *previous page* Damage to the sugar works at the Lot 14 plantation, St Vincent. The photograph was taken following the eruption of May 1902, but it is not known how much of this damage had been done during the eruption or during the hurricane of 1898. Photograph by Tempest Anderson, 1904. © York Museums Trust.

Figure 69 *previous page* Image of Bunker's Hill, Richmond, St Vincent, on 30 May 1902. This lies within the area described as having suffered total destruction. Notice that many coconut palms have lost their leaves but are still upright, while the ground is covered in a thick layer of volcanic ash. Photograph by Tempest Anderson. © York Museums Trust.

Figure 70 False colour air photo of the summit crater of St Vincent in April 1977. The crater contains a lava dome that was extruded into the lake in 1971. Oxford, Bodleian Library, Directorate of Overseas Surveys air photo 606141624 no. 094. Flight line 163/VC/16.

self-sufficient and to grow economic crops for export. In the first weeks of the crisis, Robert Llewelyn was swayed by requests from the estates owners for compensation for losses. He was soon rebuked by Chamberlain, who insisted that the emergency funds be used to provide relief to those people suffering or for purchasing lands for resettlement. The sugar industry never recovered, and instead the eruption hastened the transition to new crops: sea-island cotton and bananas.

The volcano had three more bursts of activity, in mid-May, September and October 1902, and a last gasp in March 1903 when Barbados was once more covered in ash. Some of the best 'time-stamped' samples from each of these eruptions actually come from Barbados, where government scientists worked hard to collect the ash as it fell, so that they could assess its potential as a fertilizer. The Reverend Norton Watson, vicar of St Martin's, laid out a sheet in the vicarage garden, scooping up the volcanic dust every hour until each fall of ash ceased. He sent his samples on to John Flett in London, and today they sit in Flett's archive in London's Natural History Museum.

After 1903, Soufrière St Vincent returned to a state of quiescence which wasn't disturbed until 1971, when a remarkably quiet eruption built a new lava dome within the flooded crater of the volcano (Figure 70). This new activity, and the subsequent unrest on the nearby island of Guadeloupe in 1976, helped to stimulate the expansion of networks of volcano-monitoring instruments to detect earthquakes and changes in ground levels. This investment paid off quickly, with the rapid onset of new activity in 1979.

The 1979 eruptions began with only a very short period of unrest, starting with a strong local earthquake on 12 April. Eruptive activity began with a series of short-lived but violent explosions that lofted a series of ash plumes high into the sky on 13 April 1979, Good Friday. This heralded two weeks of vigorous activity that peaked with an 18-kilometre-high plume on 17 April and ended with the cessation of measurable seismicity on 29 April. After this, the eruption switched to the quiet extrusion of lava, slowly forming the dome that still sits in the crater today. The 1979 eruption caused much disruption, with 20,000 people evacuated to shelters, but no direct loss of life.

## The destruction of St Pierre, Martinique

On 8 May 1902, 150 kilometres away from St Vincent and one day later, Mont Pelée joined the fray. A little before 8 am, Pelée erupted with devastating and well-documented consequences. Searing clouds of ash descended rapidly from the mountain, laying waste to the seaside town of St Pierre. A French traveller, Comte de Fitz-James, had taken a rowing boat from St Pierre to visit a village, Precheur, on the other side of the harbour that had been damaged in an eruption on 3 May.

> As we made our way across the water we more than half-faced Mont Pelée, which was throwing off a heavy cloud of smoke, steam and ashes. Not a ripple was to be seen on the face of the water. The rumblings from the bowels of the mountain were majestic in tone. [Then] there came an explosion that was beyond anything that ever before happened. The breath of fire swept down upon the city and water front with all of the force that could have been given to it by a cannon. Cinders were shot into our face with stinging effect. The air was filled with flame. Involuntarily we raised our hands to protect our faces. I noticed the same gesture when I saw the bodies of the victims on shore; arms had been raised and the hands were extended with the palms outward, a gesture that indicated dread and horror.[98]

From a population of 28,000 there were just three survivors: a prisoner, Louis-Auguste Cyparis, saved by being incarcerated in a subterranean prison; Léon Compère-Léandre, a shoe-maker; and Havivra Da Ifrile, a little girl rescued out at sea. The destruction at St Pierre was particularly terrible, laying waste as it did to a city of 28,000 inhabitants, and causing death and destruction on a scale not seen before in any eruption in the northern hemisphere. Even ships that were anchored in the harbour offshore from St Pierre weren't spared from the whirlwind of fire, as they were engulfed by hot ash clouds.

The aftermath of these two terrible eruptions provided a tremendous stimulus for scientific research into volcanoes – in much the same way that the earlier eruptions of Santorini (in 1866) and Krakatoa (in 1883) did, as well as the later eruptions of Mt St Helens (1980) and Pinatubo (1991). Teams of scientists from the United Kingdom, France and the United States were sent out by their respective national academies to conduct studies into what had happened. The Royal Society dispatched John Flett, a young geologist who later became Director of the British Geological Survey, and the volcano photographer Tempest Anderson (see Chapter 2). Their transcription of eyewitness accounts and geological observations provide astonishing details of the events as they unfolded. Their samples can still be found in museum archives today, capturing moments in the volcanic eruptions that are no longer preserved in situ. The scientific legacy was an understanding of the process by which devastating hot pyroclastic density currents, or 'burning clouds', form during eruptions – a phenomenon first captured on film by Alfred Lacroix on Martinique (Figure 71) – and of their dreadful consequences for the people and communities unfortunate enough to have experienced them.

Figure 71   Ash cloud over Martinique, 1904. From A. Lacroix, *La Montagne Pelée et ses Eruptions*, Masson et cie, Paris, 1904. Oxford, Bodleian Library, 18823 c.8, frontispiece.

# CHAPTER 7
## Detecting the next volcanic eruption

THE PAST 150 YEARS have seen a dramatic change in our ability to measure activity at volcanoes, whether they are dormant or in eruption. New instruments have been designed that can measure earthquakes, sound, gases and heat at volcanoes, either from the ground or from space. Many of the world's most active volcanoes are bristling with sensors, beaming back their measurements by cable, Wi-Fi or mobile phone to the nearest observatory. Fleets of satellites form a global network, a little like a remote observatory, with on-board sensors detecting changes in the shape of the volcano or in the amounts of heat and quantities of different gases escaping out of it. In recent years, new global networks of instruments have all been used to spot eruptions that otherwise may have gone unnoticed: the global lightning network; the global infrasound arrays, used to detect very low frequency sounds that bounce around the globe after nuclear explosions; and the ocean buoy network used to measure sounds in the deep sound channels of the world's oceans.

Today, scientists can measure the properties of rocks deep beneath our feet, and start to try to test ideas about where molten magma might form or accumulate before an eruption. All of this should be good news for the people who live near volcanoes, or for visitors attracted to their steaming slopes (Figure 72). But there is still a long way to go. Just because we can measure things doesn't mean that we can understand what those measurements mean. And since much of the history of the study of volcanoes has focused on their behaviour when they are erupting, we have a very poor idea of how some volcanoes behave when they are not erupting. Equally, at volcanoes that have been long-dormant, and are perhaps very quiet, we may have very little idea of the clues that might signal that an eruption is about to happen.

Figure 72  The perils of volcano tourism and an unexpected eruption on Vesuvius. *The Descent*, coloured lithograph by G. Dura, 1850. Wellcome Library, London.

Lit. Gatti e Dura d.t. Gigante 19.

Our capacity to record volcanic activity has also been transformed. Before the arrival of the camera, visual records of eruptions could only ever be snapshots, drawn as fast as the sketcher was able, or composite images that captured some of the features of the eruption. Today, streaming video and web-cams mean that we can watch events unfurl from our desktop computers and mobile devices, and then we can go back and watch them frame by frame. Weather satellites capture the spread of ash clouds and their tracks around the globe. While this flood of digital information may mean that we can see more quickly what is happening, it poses new problems for storage and archiving. No one has yet designed a system for quickly reducing these data flows to the 'key performance indicators' that might best help describe what is happening now and diagnose what might happen in the future.

The rapid and ready availability of digital imagery, and the ease of sharing this information widely, for example through social media, is not always a good thing. Misinformation can spread just as quickly as any other sort of information, and in the hurly-burly of a rapidly unfolding event, recycled images of past events can quickly be adopted as 'true likenesses' of the new. As with imagery from past eruptions, it can be hard to detect embellishment or exaggeration in the heat of the moment.

## Santorini, Greece

As an example of what it is possible to detect at volcanoes that are starting to show unrest, we shall take a look at Santorini volcano, Greece. Santorini, also known as Thera, is a spectacular group of islands gathered around a huge flooded crater in the Aegean Sea (Figure 73). It is one of the best exposed and most accessible volcanic islands in the world, and has played an important part in the development of the science of volcanoes. Santorini was well known to the natural historians of the ancient world, and has continued growing in eruptions for at least the past 3,000 years.

From satellites, the arcuate form of the main islands of Santorini is easy to see. Look more closely and you'll see the inconspicuous dark shadows of the two youngest volcanic islands – the 'burnt' or Kameni islands – that lie within the great flooded caldera. These islands form the literal 'tip' of the present-day volcano, which has risen within Santorini's caldera since the last major explosive eruption, the Minoan eruption

Figure 73　The island of Santorini, Greece. From Cristoforo Buondelmonti's *Liber insularum archipelagi,* c. 1420, in a copy dated 1474. Oxford, Bodleian Library, MS. Canon. Misc. 280, fol3. 23v–24r.

reddit, hac vox arenarium incas?ibus demon-
ui frater & dei filius de bello troiano reuerteris
applicuit, marisq procellis & nausea lacessitus
occubuit, cui usq in hodiernum honorabile
sepulchrum epitaphio sculpto condidimus.
circuit in valla ?pxxx. cuius in medio ?dus
nobilissimus arenium aquas radianalium
sulphuris existerui incrauitur, inquo ?ortis
plenus apparet dorati, aliquibus. Versus ?o ori-
tera & tenera ciuitas eleuatur munitissima.
inqua euenit mancipii empto ? tempore posta
aliter. hinc inde in laboris accidentes castel-
lum deus infervuat & dorarita loca occidit.
hac aut cum paçent circumstantes armisquiri-
bus totis elapsis diebus inexpugnabile uice-
runt castrum. z mancipia ad natura dica-
dere. Cibalesuu roperir adoratur: que sculp-
ta tenturis priolis lapidis ornata cum corona
turridera. & galli sequentes z leones taium
trahebant: que clauem ? manu gestabat: ?
abalesi terra dr: quia terra ? aeris, in ro?is ar immun-
dus rotatur z nobilis? est leonis, ut ostendat
materia putas: eisui senitas materia sis-
citur affectioni. Lapidis priolis ueritas ig-
ceum est uar cui metallos. Galli q eius sar-
detur castrari erunt: quia ?cosabant dicebat
Turris coronata: quia in ?eis sunt ciuitas
& castra. clauis: quia ?euro ? trie terra apidi
z ? hyerae clauditur. Ad occiduu oppidum
erat pollona: quo coram scopuli q rasule
? aute appaet uulte z hinc inde sparse
? totum.

Scandi de ailo ?c ad insulam ?yprim
accedamus. Zephanus grece latine si-
lubo: ?ii?q peam accesforis monte traza-
rdam altelbes mam z comitate ab ?bus
?l circuitu in id oriente ?o in monte ?ere
Zaugiau ciuitas est de nomine ?ysule
dca. Ad oriedum aut Siconisi leoruq apii
z sinus, ad meridiem portus concluditur
olim cu urbe derupta. que ?rie plangiallo
nominatur z insic?ffectu scopulaz ditam

Sypri

Seraga

Suconisi

Plangiallo
Chitam

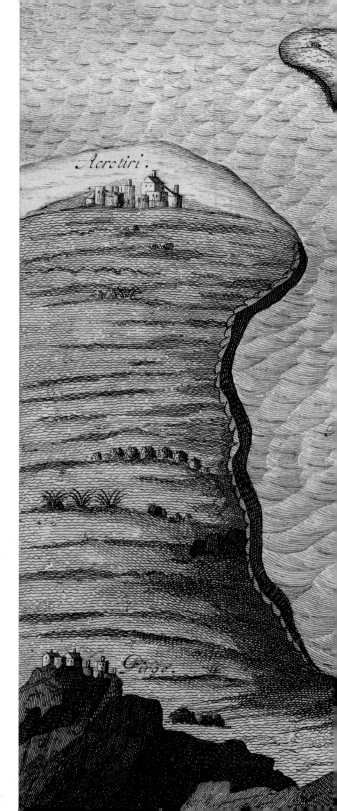

Figure 74   The 'burnt' or Kameni islands of Santorini, during the eruption of 1707–1712. *Philosophical Transactions of the Royal Society of London,* vol. 27, no. 332, 1711, pp. 354–75. Courtesy of Linda Hall Library of Science, Engineering and Technology.

ronisi.

Therasia.

Great Kammeni.

The New Island, or Black Island.

Kammeni

Scare

Apanom.

Merevigli.

of *c.*1600 BCE. Historical records and accounts from as far back as the Greek geographer Strabo suggest that there have been at least ten eruptions in and around the Kameni islands since 197 BCE. It is quite likely that there have been more that either haven't been noticed (because they were underwater) or that have been forgotten about with the passage of time. Indeed, it has been suggested that the ancient city of Cyrene, in present-day Libya, may have been founded in 630 BCE by Greeks who were escaping an earlier eruption of Thera.

The present-day Kameni islands have a volume of about 3 cubic kilometres of lava, measured from the sea floor, and must have risen at an average rate of about 1 million cubic metres per year ever since the Minoan eruption – about enough lava to fill a large football stadium. Mapping of the sea floor reveals the intricate details of the underwater shape of the Kameni islands, and allows geologists to work out the sequence of eruptions that formed them.

Since Santorini is accessible, it is quite closely observed, and there are many maps and sketches of the ways in which the volcano has changed during eruptions over the past 300 years.

The first eruption of Santorini for which we have written reports and sketches is one that began in May 1707 (Figure 74). This was described by a Jesuit priest, Father Goree:

> Five days before it appeared, viz. on the 18th May, between one and two of the clock in the afternoon there was at Santorini an earthquake, which was not violent, and continued but a moment. And in the night between the 22nd and 23rd there was also another. Add to this, that a long time before these earthquakes, the fishermen perceived an ill smell every time they passed by that place. On the 23rd May at break of Day, the new island was first discovered.[99]

Figure 75 Dramatic visualization of the eruption of Santorini, 1866. Relievo map made by Stübel, from Fritsch et al., *Santorin. The Kaimeni Islands…* 1866. Oxford, Bodleian Library, 20545 b.4, plate 30.

The seamen who found the island first thought it was an upturned boat, but then were able to climb onto it 'upon which they met with several very remarkable curiosities; among which we may reckon a sort of white stone, which cuts like bread, and a great number of fresh oysters which they found sticking to the rocks.'[100] Over the next few days the new island grew in height and breadth, and the seas around changed from a

# SANTORIN.

Fig. 1.

Pl. III.

Fig. 2.

## A Birds-eye View of the Kaimeni-Islands and the adjacent Bottom of the Sea.

Fig. 1.
Exhibiting the Configuration of the Islands before the Eruption
in 1866.

Fig. 2.
Exhibiting the same after the Eruption according to the State
of volcanic New Formation of May 30th 1866.

green to a reddish or yellowish colour 'with a stink which spreading itself over great part of Santorini made us imagine that this colour proceeded from nothing else but the sulphur with which the sea was covered'. It wasn't until 16 July, two months into the eruption, that the 'fire and smoak and great noise' appeared.[101]

This is a wonderful tale, which first describes how the ground surface was lifted up by the arrival of magma close to the surface, and then the later eruption of that magma out of a new vent at the summit of the dome of rock. One reason for thinking that this account is faithful to what happened is that it is similar to the opening stages of more recent eruptions. In January 1866, there were mild earthquakes, marked changes in the ground surface and changes in the colour of the sea before the eruption started (Figure 75), and similar patterns were observed in 1925 and 1939. With this sort of information, we can develop some simple ideas about what signs we might see in advance of a future eruption at the same volcano.

When I first visited Santorini it was hot, dusty and felt rather exotic as it was my first taste of Greece. On a summer's day, a trudge over the dark gravelly rocks of Nea Kameni, the younger and larger of the two islands, is usually exceedingly hot. The island is almost barren, apart from a few patches of lupins and some grasses. In the centre of Nea Kameni, the tourist trails circle around some shallow explosion craters, which is where you may find a few small, steamy vents, but in the dry warm air, the visible signs of activity in the craters are often a little disappointing. There are none of the dense acrid fumes that you will find in the craters of Vulcano or the Campi Flegrei in Italy, and only rather small patches of yellow sulphur or white altered ground, compared with that which you might see at White Island, New Zealand, or on Mount Etna, for example. Although it is not visible to the naked eye, this summit area is gradually leaking carbon dioxide and other volcanic gases into the atmosphere.

In January 2011, Santorini began to show the first subtle signs of stirring after many decades of quiet – or at least many decades without detectable activity. This provided a rare opportunity to track the behaviour of a volcano at the beginning of a period of unrest. Although it may seem counter-intuitive, volcanologists don't really have a terribly good idea of how volcanoes behave in the long hiatuses between eruptions. Most of the time, resources are devoted to studying volcanoes that are about to erupt, are already erupting or that have recently erupted, rather than the

Figure 76 Model of the vertical movement of Santorini during 2011–12, caused by the intrusion of a pool of magma at 4 kilometres depth. The red dot shows the location of the centre of the magma chamber. © Michelle Parks.

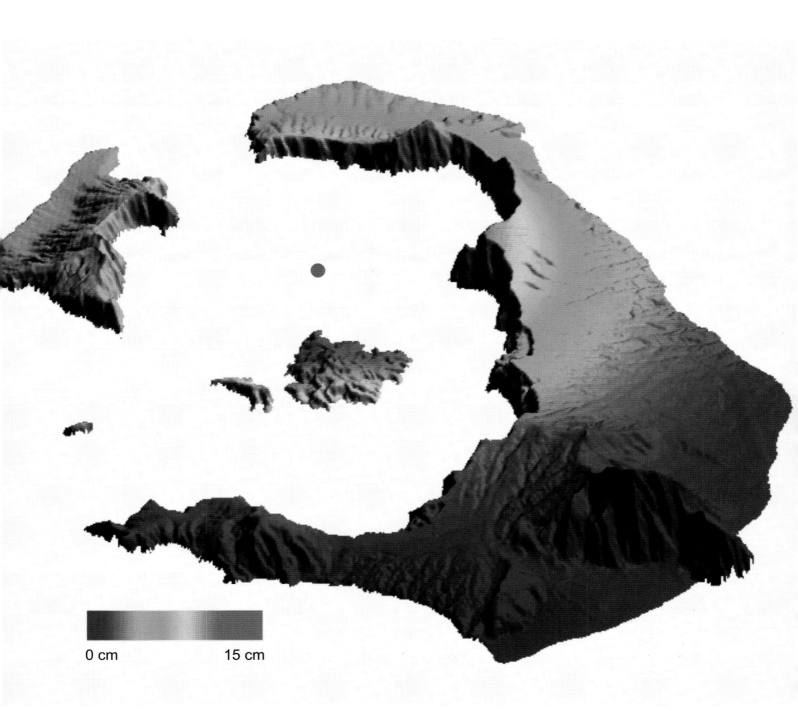

slumbering volcanoes that might be thought to pose rather less of an immediate hazard.

The first signs of something stirring came from tiny earthquakes that began to be detected beneath the centre of the volcano. These were too small to be felt, but were large enough to be picked up by the local Greek network of seismometers, designed to detect earthquakes. For the first time, there were more earthquakes occurring beneath Santorini than at its near-neighbour, an underwater volcano called Kolombos bank, 15 kilometres away. Shortly afterwards, we began to see signs of ground movement from radar instruments on satellites and from sensitive ground-based global positioning system instruments, showing that the whole volcano was beginning to swell. The northern end of Nea Kameni was rising out of the sea at a rate of a few centimetres per year, and all of the circling islands of Santorini were moving outwards, away from the centre of the caldera. Apart from a small number of sharp earthquakes that were felt locally, there was nothing significant that would have been noticed without monitoring technology. In the harbour of Nea Kameni, where tourist boats pull up against the remains of the 1570 lava cone, the small changes in land surface might have been seen by a keen observer, as the old tide marks rose out of the sea – but who would have known to look?

The way in which a volcano swells tells us about where the pressure source lies. Imagine blowing up a balloon that is buried within a sandpit. If the balloon is very deep, the disturbance at the surface will be quite small and spread out. If it is shallow, the sand will bulge dramatically over the top of the expanding balloon. Computer simulations of this swelling suggested that the cause of the unrest was the arrival of a small blob of molten rock about 4 kilometres beneath the volcano, somewhere beneath the northern part of Santorini's sea-filled caldera (Figure 76).

From early 2011, our instruments traced out the gradual changes at the surface as 20 million cubic metres of molten rock slowly squeezed into this subterranean reservoir – enough to fill Wembley football stadium about twenty times over. Hundreds of very small earthquakes continued to rattle the volcano until January 2012, when they began to peter out. There were also subtle changes in the gases leaking out of the summit craters of Nea Kameni islands. The concentrations of these gases were so low that they had to be measured directly during field campaigns. By making repeated measurements across a grid using a small bell jar connected to a pump and a sensor, we were able to measure the small amounts of carbon dioxide escaping to the atmosphere from the surface of Nea Kameni. Early in 2011, the pattern of soil–gas carbon dioxide changed, as new gas percolated into and through the shallow parts of the volcano towards the surface. This gas pulse then solwly declined, until by April 2012, all of the signs were that the volcanic system beneath Santorini had returned to a quiet state. If this short and subtle episode of unrest had happened more than thirty years ago, it would not have been detected – without the satellite instruments and local seismometer network there would have been too few clues that anything might be amiss.

New batches of magma must be arriving repeatedly in the magma storage systems beneath slumbering volcanoes. It seems likely that this is how volcanoes slowly prepare for a future eruption, growing drip by drip until eventually they are ready to erupt. But we have no way of working out how often these events might have happened in the past, or of what they might tell us about the future, simply because they are too subtle and too transient to leave any trace in either the historical or geological records of volcanoes. The geological and historical records of past eruptions have strong parallels: both have detection thresholds, below which little or nothing will be recorded or preserved. In both, records are also likely to be biased towards the extraordinary.

## Why can't we predict volcanic eruptions?

Every year, a handful of volcanoes return to life after a long period of repose. Sometimes, there may be an extended warning, but at other times, there may be very little. The reawakening of a long-dormant volcano poses one of the biggest challenges to volcanologists, simply because these volcanoes will not usually have a well-established track record of behaviour. In the past fifty years, several of the most troublesome eruptions have been at volcanoes that have erupted for the first time in recorded history. The two most significant explosive eruptions of the past forty years both occurred at volcanoes that were barely known before a fanfare of earthquakes announced their arrival: El Chichón, Mexico, in March 1982 and Pinatubo, Philippines, in June 1991. At Pinatubo, only three months elapsed between the first felt earthquakes and the main paroxysmal phase of the eruption – just long enough to identify the potential hazards posed by the volcano and to start to prepare the millions of people who lived within reach of the ash clouds and mudflows that were expected to accompany an eruption.

Indonesia is the most volcanically-active region of the world, with over 140 known volcanoes, 78 of which have erupted in historical times. Activity at many of these volcanoes has waxed and waned, with episodes of activity separated by decades to centuries of quiet (Figure 77). One of the most dangerous volcanoes in eruption, at the time of writing, is Mount Sinabung, a large stratovolcano surrounded by farming lands on the Indonesian island of Sumatra. In August 2010 the first historical eruption of Sinabung ended at least 400 years of dormancy. Since then, activity at Sinabung has waxed and waned, with repeated episodes of violent eruption triggering large-scale evacuations of several tens of thousands of people from communities at the foot of the volcano. The most damaging activity at Sinabung is caused by the break-off and collapse of the hot, viscous front of a slowly extruding lava flow. This hot rock avalanche quickly transforms into rapidly moving pyroclastic flows that sweep off the flanks of the volcano. Sinabung is now well monitored by the Indonesian national volcano monitoring agency, but the variable intensity of the eruption, its long duration and its accessibility mean that people often enter the formal exclusion zone, whether to tend to their fields and livestock, to recover belongings or for tourism and other reasons. There have been several times when rapid changes in activity have led to multiple fatalities, as people are engulfed in searing clouds of hot ash. Eruptions of this style, like that at Unzen, Japan, in 1991 (Chapter 1) and Montserrat in June 1997 (Chapter 6), are inherently unpredictable, even when closely monitored.

In April 2015, Calbuco volcano in Chile burst back to life with less than two hours' warning after over forty years of silence (see Figure 8). In the era of global satellite monitoring and with proliferating networks of instruments on the ground, why can we still not predict volcanic eruptions? Our capacity to watch, record and comment once an eruption has started (Figure 78) is not yet matched by our ability to anticipate what might happen next at a restless but dormant volcano. Using a medical analogy, we might now have a very clear sense of the 'state of a volcano' based on observations of many other volcanoes around the world, but if we don't know the prior history of a particular volcano, and with no way of taking the equivalent of a biopsy from a restless volcano,

Figure 77 The steaming summit crater of Guntur or 'thunder' volcano, Java, Indonesia, dormant since 1847. A large mudslide in October 1800 overwhelmed several villages and killed many people; an eruption in June 1825 caused extensive damage to coffee plantations and buried rice fields under volcanic ash. Johannes Muller, *Beschreibung der Insel Java*, 1860. Oxford, Bodleian Library, (OC) 246 h.70, opp. p. 109.

our capacity to work out what is going on is always going to be limited. For example, some volcanoes stay completely quiet and then erupt violently without warning, while others are noisy, but have a moment of calm before eruption.

While we can't yet safely drill into a rumbling volcano, the deposits from past eruptions may contain the information we need about what happened in the build-up to those eruptions. Any volcanic activity that involves the eruption of solid materials (or materials that will become solid) will have the potential to leave a trace in the geological rock record, whether as a layer of volcanic ash preserved in a lake, peat bog or soil, or the frozen remnants of lava flow or similar. As long as these deposits are not too badly affected by weathering and alteration processes, they can be collected and analysed. The physical nature of the samples and what they are made of (minerals, glass) can be used to understand where and how they formed, and how they were erupted. However, the geological record is imperfect and the deposits of many smaller to moderate eruptions are only transient and unlikely to be preserved. But for some eruptions from the eighteenth to the twentieth century, fresh samples collected at the time can still be found in museum archives, from date-stamped lavas erupted from Vesuvius to date- and time-stamped ash samples collected on land or at sea during the 1902 eruptions of the Soufrière of St Vincent and Mont Pelée. These are carefully retained and available for modern analysis in ways that would not have been imagined at the time. None of these samples exist anymore 'in the wild'– they have been either buried or washed away or have rotted.

Explosive eruptions typically throw out large quantities of ejecta – the frozen and disrupted remnants of the eviscerated magma reservoir. This often includes pumice, a light and frothy rock that is a network of tiny glassy tubes, sheets and strands, with a void space now filled with air and that would have contained volcanic gas just before eruption. Other components include crystals of different minerals that grew at depth as the magma cooled and started to solidify, perhaps for decades or centuries.

Bubbles of gas are thought to be the main agent that causes explosive eruptions. At depth, when fresh magma first arrives beneath the volcano, it usually contains quantities of dissolved gases, such as water and carbon dioxide. As the magma freezes, the gases remain dissolved in a smaller and smaller amount of melt, until eventually the melt becomes saturated and bubbles of gas start to form. From this point, the pressure inside the volcano will begin to build, and eventually, the rocks around the magma

Figure 78  Peering into the crater of Stromboli, a volcano that has erupted repeatedly for at least 2,000 years, but still has the capacity to surprise. 'Strombolian' eruptions are considered to be driven by the bursting of large gas bubbles at the top of a long conduit of magma. From Count de Bylandt Palstercamp's *Theorie de volcans*, 1836. Oxford, Bodleian Library, Mason Z 394, plate 14.

chamber will crack and the bubbly magma will rise through the cracks to the surface, starting an eruption. Before, during and after eruptions the gases responsible for the activity can escape from the magma, leaving little trace of their former presence.

So how can we detect the point at which the magma starts to grow bubbles? This is where forensic volcanology comes in. As magmas freeze, the crystals formed at different times will capture snapshots of the state of the magma reservoir beneath the volcano. With some good fortune, it is sometimes possible to go and find these crystals after an eruption and piece together the sequence of events. Some minerals that are common in volcanic rock have turned out to be particularly good time capsules. The green olivine crystals that are often found in basalts – and seen by William Hamilton at Vesuvius and Constance Gordon-Cumming at Hawaii, among others – can be used to tell us about the temperatures at depth, where they first formed. Often, olivine crystals may trap tiny blobs of liquid magma deep in the bowels of the volcano. With luck, these tiny blobs will freeze to glass droplets when the olivine crystal is eventually ejected from the volcano and can then be used to find out more about the magmas at depth.

In the Campi Flegrei volcanic system in the Bay of Naples (Chapter 1), there have been repeated explosive eruptions over the past 40,000 years, but only one for which historical records exist: the 1538 CE Monte Nuovo eruption (Chapter 1). One common feature of many of these magmas is that they contain small amounts of a calcium phosphate mineral called apatite, which is rather like tooth enamel, only grown at high temperature from a magma. Apatite has the fortunate property that as it grows it preserves information about how much water, chlorine, fluorine and sulphur – the species that make up volcanic gas – are in the magma. Apatite is resistant to change, so its composition today will record information about the state of the volcano at the time the mineral was last in contact with magma. Studies of apatite from Campi Flegrei show that in recent eruptions, the magma in which the apatite grew didn't contain bubbles of steam until perhaps a few weeks or months before eruption. Since many eruptions are thought to be caused by the formation and growth of bubbles, the best signals of an impending eruption at this sort of volcano might be found by looking at patterns of ground movement (changing pressure) and in the compositions of gases escaping out of the volcano (Figure 79) – leaking out of the bubbly magma. Taking a forensic look at past eruptions by using samples collected from those eruptions is one of the best

Figure 79 Collecting volcanic gas from the steaming sulphur-coated summit of Vulcano, the Aeolian Islands. Lipari Island is in the background. © David M. Pyle.

tools available to geologists, and is a way to identify the monitoring signals that offer clues to future behaviour and move us a step closer to being able to predict volcanic eruptions. In a similar vein, the written and visual records of past eruptions (Figure 80) contain an untapped wealth of information about the ways that volcanoes change during eruption, and the wider consequences of their activity; information that could help to mitigate the impacts of future eruptions.

## What if there was a supervolcanic eruption?

For reasons that are perhaps obvious, interest in global geophysical catastrophes strike a chord with the public imagination, and none more so than Yellowstone and supervolcanoes. The term 'supervolcano' was popularized as the name of dramatic imagination of what might happen in a future eruption of Yellowstone, a caldera volcano in Wyoming that has had three colossal explosive eruptions, and many smaller ones, in the past 2 million years. The term has come to signify a catastrophic volcanic eruption; in the same way that Krakatoa came to symbolize volcanic disaster a century ago (see Chapter 5). Even though the chance of an eruption on a

Figure 80  Early volcano monitoring: sketches of the progressive changes in the summit cone of Vesuvius, drawn by William Hamilton, 1773. W. Hamilton, *Observations on Mount Vesuvius, Mount Etna...* 1773. Oxford, Bodleian Library, Vet. A5 e.215, fig. 19.

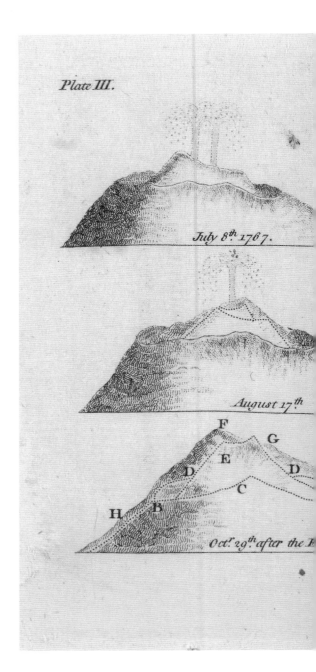

*Plate III.*

*July 8th 1767.*

*August 17th*

F
G
E
D
D
C
H
B
*Octr 29th after the E...*

*July 25.th*            *August 6.th*

*September 3.d*        *Oct.r 18.th day before the Eruption.*

## The ancient Crater of Mount Vesuvius,

### With the gradual increase of the little Mountain within the Crater.

The exteriour black line marks each increase, & the interiour dotted line shews the state of the little Mountain before that increase, so that the dotted line in the Drawing of Oct.r 18.th shews the Size of the little Mountain July 8.th the little spot A. marks where the lava came out some days before the great Eruption. B.C.D. mark the ancient Crater & E. the little Mountain the day before the Eruption. F.G. is the present Crater, & the exteriour black line H.F.G. the present shape of the top of Mount Vesuvius. Since May last the Mountain is increased from B. to E. which is near 200 feet. - - - - - - - - - - - - - - - - - - - - -

'supervolcano' scale – involving the explosive eruption of over 1,000 cubic kilometres of ash and pumice – in our lifetimes might be vanishingly small, it wouldn't take an eruption of that scale to have a global impact. Tambora, in 1815 (Chapter 5), disgorged about a tenth of this amount of material 200 years ago and left an unequivocal signal in global environmental records. Setting aside the medium-term environmental consequences, a repeat of a Tambora-scale event would have immediate consequences for global transport, trade and financial flows on a scale not realized by any previous volcanic eruption, and likely exceeding the impacts of the world's two most recent geophysical catastrophes: the 2004 Indian Ocean earthquake and tsunami, and the 2011 Tohoku earthquake and tsunami in Japan.

Two recent events on different sides of the Atlantic might help us to imagine the scale of a future supervolcanic eruption. In April 2010, a vast swathe of European airspace, from Iceland to Ireland and from Spain to Poland, was closed on and off for five days as ash from the Icelandic volcano Eyjafjallajökull drifted slowly through European airspace. This tiny cloud left barely a trace of volcanic ash on the ground, but paralysed the global travel network in a way that few had imagined might be possible. Had this been a supervolcanic eruption, that entire area, the whole of Europe, would have been coated with ash 10 centimetres thick, a fine, grey–white powder that would billow around your ankles as you struggled to walk – that's paralysis.

A second example comes from October 2012 and the eastern seaboard of the United States. The world could only stand by and watch as storm system Sandy, which had already wreaked havoc in Cuba, Haiti and Jamaica, grew to a size that threatened to engulf the entire east coast from Florida to New York, and drove wind fields from Newfoundland to the Great Lakes. When superstorm Sandy made landfall, the storm system was over 1,000 kilometres across and visible from far out in space. Replace the winds and the rain with ash, and you have the scale of a supervolcanic ash cloud, such as the one that would have rolled across North America after the last great eruption of Yellowstone. Both events also show something of our capacity, as humans, to observe these unfolding events from space, and, in the case of Sandy, to run sophisticated simulations of weather systems that actually forecast the land fall and storm surge correctly. But then this shouldn't be a great surprise – we have 100 years of detailed observations and a list of great Atlantic storms that sound like an extended family that have helped meteorologists build their forecast 'skill'. The next supervolcanic eruption won't afford us the same luxury, with only one globally significant eruption of the satellite era, Pinatubo 1991, available as a calibration.

While colossal explosive volcanic events with a global reach are a real phenomenon, with a well-preserved geological record of physical traces of buried volcanic ash, they are also of a scale that has never been seen during the historical era. So what might the next eruption of a supervolcano look like? Although there have been no supervolcanic eruptions for about 26,000 years (since the Oruanui eruption of Taupo volcano in New Zealand), from field studies and computer simulations we have a fair idea of what the immediate consequences of one might be. The immediate physical consequences are predictable: an area of up to several thousand kilometres from the volcano will be buried under volcanic ash, disrupting lives and livelihoods. Transportation, communications and life's essentials – fresh water, food, warmth, shelter, energy – will be put under considerable stress, if not removed entirely. The knock-on consequences for the global economy of a future supervolcanic eruption might be hard to predict, but it is difficult to imagine that the short-term consequences would be anything other than catastrophic. Beyond day one, the consequences are limited only by our imaginations – consequences uncharted in human experience.

Humans seem to have a great capacity for resilience, an ability to overcome challenges posed by natural processes, to bounce back from natural disasters and to do their best to record and understand them. This much is clear if one compares the period of time in which modern humans (*Homo sapiens*) have existed and a short catalogue of the major events of the natural world which they appear to have survived: the catastrophic eruption of Toba, Indonesia, 74,000 years ago; the Last Glaciation, from 30,000 to 18,000 years ago.

Worrying about the next supervolcano eruption might be a little academic when we haven't even learnt how to live with volcanoes and eruptions of a much smaller scale (Figure 81). But there is much that we can do to improve our capacity to live safely with volcanoes. By remembering, analysing and using the experiences of those who have been affected by volcanic activity in the past, we shall be able to prepare for a more resilient future.

Figure 81   Paroxysmal eruption of Vesuvius seen from Naples. Eighteenth-century gouache. Wellcome Library, London.

# GAZETTEER OF ERUPTIONS

Dates of notable eruptions of selected volcanoes mentioned in the text.

| Date | Volcano | Notes |
|---|---|---|
| 24 August 79 | Vesuvius, Italy | Destroys Pompeii and Herculaneum |
| 29 September 1538 | Monte Nuovo, Italy | Start of the eruption |
| 16 December 1631 | Vesuvius, Italy | Start of major eruption |
| 11 March 1669 | Etna, Sicily, Italy | Start of the eruption |
| 23 May 1707 | Santorini, Greece | Start of lava-dome eruption |
| 26 March 1718 | Soufrière, St Vincent | Start of the eruption |
| 20 September 1759 | Jorullo, Mexico | Birth of the volcano |
| 8 June 1783 | Laki, Iceland | Start of major fissure eruption |
| 30 January 1811 | Sabrina island, São Miguel, Azores | Start of the eruption |
| 27 April 1812 | Soufrière, St Vincent | Climactic phase |
| 10 April 1815 | Tambora, Indonesia | Climactic phase |
| 28 June 1831 | Campi Flegrei Mar de Sicilia, Italy | Birth of Graham Island |
| 26 April 1872 | Vesuvius, Italy | First photograph |
| 26 August 1883 | Krakatoa, Indonesia | Climactic phase |
| 7 May 1902 | Soufrière, St Vincent | Climactic phase |
| 8 May 1902 | Mount Pelée, Martinique | Climactic phase |
| 7 April 1906 | Vesuvius, Italy | Climactic phase |
| 20 February 1943 | Parícutin, Mexico | Birth of the volcano |
| 18 March 1944 | Vesuvius, Italy | Start of the most recent eruption |
| 8 November 1963 | Surtsey, Iceland | Start of the eruption |
| 18 May 1980 | Mount St Helens, USA | Climactic phase |
| 28 March 1982 | El Chichón, Mexico | Major explosive eruption |
| 3 January 1983 | Kilauea, Hawaii | Start of the continuing eruption |
| 25 March 1984 | Mauna Loa, Hawaii | Start of the eruption |
| 21 May 1991 | Unzen, Japan | Lava-dome extrusion begins |
| 15 June 1991 | Pinatubo, Philippines | Climatic phase, major explosive eruption |
| 18 July 1995 | Soufrière Hills Volcano, Montserrat | Start of the eruption |
| 20 March 2010 | Eyjafjallajökull, Iceland | Start of the eruption |
| 27 August 2010 | Sinabung, Indonesia | Start of the eruption |
| 4 June 2011 | Puyehue Cordon-Caulle, Chile | Start of the eruption |
| 29 August 2014 | Bardarbunga, Iceland | Start of the Holuhraun eruption |
| 27 September 2014 | Ontake, Japan | Fatal explosion |
| 22 April 2015 | Calbuco, Chile | Start of the eruption |

# NOTES

1    Archibald Geikie, 'On modern denudation', *Transactions of the Geological Society of Glasgow*, vol. 3, 1871, p. 188.

2    Bertrand Russell, *History of Western Philosophy*, Routledge, London, 2004, p. 60.

3    Ovid, *Metamorphoses*, Book XV 335–379, trans. A.D. Melville, Oxford University Press, Oxford, 1998, p. 362.

4    Pliny the Younger, *Letters, Volume I: Books 1–7*, trans. Betty Radice. Loeb Classical Library 55. Harvard University Press, Cambridge, MA, 1969. Book VI, Letter XVI, p. 427.

5    Ibid. p. 429.

6    Ibid. pp. 431–3.

7    Pliny the Younger, *Letters, Volume I: Books 1–7*, trans. Betty Radice. Loeb Classical Library 55. Harvard University Press, Cambridge, MA, 1969. Book VI, Letter XX, p. 441.

8    Ibid. p. 443.

9    Ibid. p. 445.

10    Ibid. p. 447.

11    J. Logan Lobley, *Mount Vesuvius: A descriptive, historical and geological account of the volcano and its surroundings*, Roger and Drowley, London, 1889, pp. 362–5.

12    Denis O'Donoghue, *Brendaniana: St Brendan the Voyager in story and legend*, Browne and Nolan, Dublin, 1895, 2nd edn, p. 161.

13    Ibid. p. 162.

14    Translated from J.A. St John, *The history of the manners of the Ancient Greeks*, Richard Bentley, London, 1844, p. 357.

15    Sebastian Münster, *Cosmographiae universalis*, Henricus Petrus, Basel, 1550. p. 6.

16    Ibid. p. 1113.

17    Ibid. p. 6.

18    Athanasius Kircher, *The Vulcano's or mountains vomiting fire, famous in the World; with their remarkables*, J. Derby, London, 1669, p. 1.

19    Sean Cocco, *Watching Vesuvius*, University of Chicago Press, Chicago, 2012, p. 141, from the preface to Athanasius Kircher's *Subterraneus Mundi*.

20    William Bromley, *Remarks in the grand tour of France and Italy, performed by a person of quality, in the year 1691*. John Nutt, London, 1705, 2nd edn, p. 215.

21    Ibid.

22    W.E. Knowles Middleton, 'The 1669 eruption of Mount Etna: Francesco d'Arezzo on the vitreous nature of lava', *Archives of Natural History*, 1982, vol. 11, pp. 99–102.

23    Earl of Winchilsea, *A true and exact relation of the late prodigious earthquake and eruption of Mount Etna or Monte-Gibello*, T. Newcomb, London, 1669, pp. 4–5.

24    W. Hamilton, 'Two letters from the Hon, William Hamilton, His Majesty's Envoy Extraordinary at Naples, to the Earl of Morton, President of the Royal Society containing an account of the last eruption of Mount Vesuvius', *Philosophical Transactions of the Royal Society*, vol. 57, 1767, pp. 192–200.

25    Jane Waldie, *Sketches descriptive of Italy in the years 1816 and 1817, with a brief account of travels in various parts of France and Switzerland in the same years*, John Murray, London, 1820, vol. 3, p. 166.

26    Ibid. p. 167.

27   Charles Daubeny, 'Some account of the eruption of Vesuvius, which occurred in the month of August 1834', *Philosophical Transactions, Royal Society of London*, 1835, vol. 125, pp. 153–9.

28   Frank A. Perret, *The Vesuvius eruption of 1906: study of a volcanic cycle*, Carnegie Institute of Washington, Washington DC, 1924, p.. 49.

29   Letter from Joseph Wright to Richard Wright, 11 November 1774, quoted in James Hamilton, *Volcano*, Reaktion Books, London, 2012, p. 78.

30   James Boswell, *Boswell's Life of Johnson*. Ed. George Hill, 2nd edn, Clarendon Press, Oxford. 1964–1971. vol. 4: *The Life (1780–1784)*, p. 324.

31   John W. Judd, *Volcanoes: what they are and what they teach*, Kegan, Paul, Trench and Co., London, 1881. p. 24.

32   Letter from Tempest Anderson to James Bryce, 22 May 1913. Oxford, Bodleian Library, MS. Bryce 22, fol. 33.

33   Conrad Gessner, *De rerum fossilium, lapidum et gemmarum*, Tiguri, 1565, p. 20.

34   Sam Foley, 'An account of the Giants Caus-Way in the North of Ireland', *Philosophical Transactions*, vol. 18, 1694, pp. 170–82.

35   Molyneux, 1698, 'A letter… containing some additional observations on the Giants Causeway in Ireland', *Philosophical Transactions*, vol. 20, 1698, pp. 209–23.

36   R.E. Raspe, LIV. 'A letter from Mr R.E. Raspe F.R.S. to M. Maty, M.D.Sec.R.S. containing a short account of some Basalt Hills in Hassia', *Philosophical Transactions*, vol. 61, 1771, p. 581.

37   R.E. Raspe, pp. 580–3.

38   Uno von Troil, *Letters on Iceland &c*, G. Perrin, Dublin, 1780. p. 288.

39   Ibid. p. 285.

40   William Hamilton, 'A letter from Sir William Hamilton K.B. F.R.S. to Sir John Pringle, Bart. P.R.S. giving an account of certain traces of volcanos on the Banks of the Rhine', *Philosophical Transactions*, vol. 68, 1778, pp. 1–6.

41   Lazzaro Spallanzani, *Travels in the Two Sicilies etc.*, G. G. and. J. Robinson, London, 1798, vol. 3, pp. 390–402.

42   William Dampier, *A voyage to New Holland &c. in the year 1699*, James Knapton, London, 1703, vol. 3, part I, p. A3.

43   William Dampier, *Continuation of a voyage to New Holland &c. in the year 1699*, James Knapton, London, 1709, vol. 3, part II, p. 88.

44   Ibid. p. 144.

45   Ibid. p. 145.

46   Johann Forster, *Observations made during a voyage round the world*, Nicholas Thomas, Harriet Guest, Michael Dettelbach (eds), University of Hawaii Press, Honolulu, HI, 1996, p. 101.

47   Jorge Juan and Antonio de Ulloa, *Relacion historica del viaje a la America meridional*. Antonio Marin, Madrid, 1748. Vol. 1, p. 571 (translated from the Spanish).

48   Letter from J.S. Henslow to C. Darwin, 24 August 1831. Darwin Correspondence Project, DCP-LETT-105.

49   Alexander von Humboldt, *Personal Narrative of Travels to the Equinoctial Regions of the New Continent*, translated by Maria Williams, Longman, Hurst, Rees, Orme and Brown, London, 1814, vol. 1, pp. i–iii.

50   Charles Daubeny, *A description of active and extinct volcanos, with remarks on their origin, their chemical phenomena and the character of their products*, 1826.

51   George Poulett Scrope, *Considerations on Volcanoes*, W. Phillips, London, 1825, p. vii.

52   Ibid. p. 17.

53   Ibid. p. 18.

54   Ibid. p. 30.

55  John Ledyard, *A journal of Captain Cook's last voyage to the Pacific Ocean, and in quest of a north-west passage etc.*, Nathaniel Patten, Hartford, CT, 1783. p. 123.

56  C.S. Stewart, *Journal of a residence in the Sandwich islands during the years 1823, 1824 and 1825*, H. Fisher, Son, and P. Jackson, London, 1828, 2nd edn, p. 375.

57  Ibid. p. 376.

58  Constance Gordon-Cumming, *Fire Fountains: the Kingdom of Hawaii, its volcanoes and the history of its missions*, William Blackwood and Sons, Edinburgh and London, 1883, vol. I, p. 143.

59  Ibid. p. 146.

60  Ibid. pp. 164–5.

61  Ibid. p. 167.

62  Ibid. pp. 190–1.

63  Constance Gordon-Cumming, *Fire Fountains: the Kingdom of Hawaii, its volcanoes and the history of its missions*, William Blackwood and Sons, Edinburgh and London, 1883, vol. II, pp. 235–6.

64  (Anon.), *A True and Strange Relation of Fire, which by an Eruption brake forth out of the bowels of the earth in the depth of the Sea, and made an Island of foure miles and a halfe in length, one of the Islands of the Tercera's,* etc., N. Butter and N. Bourne, London, 1639.

65  S. Tillard, 'A narrative of the eruption of a volcano in the sea off the island of St Michael', *Philosophical Transactions*, vol. 102, 1812, pp. 152–8.

66  Ibid. p. 158.

67  Daubeny, 1826, pp. 337–9.

68  George Poulett Scrope, *Volcanoes*, 2nd edn, Longmans, Green and Reader, London, 1872, pp. 81–2.

69  Diary of William Dunn 1767–95, Bodleian MS Don. c. 76 -Dunn W. Diary entries for 9, 10 July 1783.

70  W. Gilpin, *An Historical Account of the Weather during Twenty Years from 1763–1785*, Oxford, Bodleian Library, MS. Eng. misc. d. 564, pp. 69–70.

71  Ibid. pp. 71–2.

72  Benjamin Franklin, 'Meteorological imaginations and conjectures', *Memoirs of the Literary and Philosophical Society of Manchester*, December 1784, pp. 373–7.

73  Sophia Raffles, *Memoir of the life and public services of Sir Thomas Stamford Raffles*, John Murray, London, 1830, p. 243.

74  Ibid. p. 249.

75  The Weather, *The Times* (London, England), Saturday, 20 July 1816, p. 3, Issue 9892.

76  Diary of The Rev. Sampson White of Maidford, Northants, 1795–1823 – MS Eng. Misc. d.241.

77  Ibid.

78  Anon., 'Scientific Aspects of the Java Catastrophe', *Nature*, vol. 28, 1883, 437.

79  G.J. Symons, 'The Krakatoa Eruption', *Nature*, vol. 29, 1884, p. 355.

80  W.S. Bristowe, *A Book of Islands*, G. Bell and Sons, London, 1969, pp. 145–6.

81  Ibid. pp. 148–50.

82  Howard A. Fergus, *Montserrat, History of a Caribbean colony*, 2nd edn, Macmillan, Oxford, 2004. p. 196.

83  Howard A. Fergus, No Birthday Poem 25.6.2000, *Volcano Verses*, Peepal Tree Press, Leeds, 2003, p. 13.

84  Herman Francis, personal communication.

85  Daniel Defoe, 'The destruction of the isle of St Vincent', in *Romances and Narratives*, ed. George Aitken, Vol. 15/16, 1895/6, pp. 241–250.

86 Alexander Anderson, 'An account of Morne Garou, a Mountain in the Island of St Vincent, with a description of the volcano on its summit', *Philosophical Transactions*, vol. 75, 1785, pp. 16–31.

87 Diary of Hugh Perry Keane, Virginia Historical Society, VHS Mss1 K197 a 23. See also transcriptions in James Hamilton, *Volcano*, Reaktion Books, London, 2012, p. 90, and S.D. Smith, 'Volcanic Hazard in a slave society: the 1812 eruption of Mount Soufrière in St Vincent', *Journal of Historical Geography* 37, 2011, pp. 55–67.

88 Blue Book for 1813, Report from Committee on Petition of Persons interested in estates on Saint Vincent, Parliamentary Papers by Command, Cd. 182, 1813, p. 7.

89 Ibid. p. 9.

90 T. Anderson and J.S. Flett, 'Report on the Eruptions of the Soufrière in St Vincent in 1902 and on a visit to Montagne Pelée', *Philosophical Transactions*, vol. 200, 1903, p. 544.

91 Blue Book, 'Correspondence relating to the volcanic eruptions in St Vincent and Martinique in May 1902, with map and appendix', Parliamentary Paper by Command, Cd. 1201, 1903, HMSO, Darling and Son, London, §80.

92 Anderson & Flett, p. 393.

93 Blue Book for 1902 §5.

94 Ibid. §18.

95 Ibid. §25.

96 Ibid. §36.

97 Ibid. §113.

98 Charles Morris, *The volcano's deadly work*, W.E. Scull, Washington DC, 1902, pp. 157–8.

99 Goree, 'A relation of a new island which was raised up from the bottom of the sea on the 23rd of May 1707', *Philosophical Transactions*, vol. 27, 1710–1712, p. 356.

100 Ibid. p. 358.

101 Ibid. pp. 359–60.

# ACKNOWLEDGEMENTS

My work on volcanoes has been supported by many wonderful friends and collaborators around the world, and with funding from the UK Research Councils, the Leverhulme Trust, the Royal Society, the British Council and the International Association of Volcanology and Chemistry of Earth's Interior. In particular I acknowledge the NERC-ESRC project 'Strengthening Resilience in Volcanic Areas', and the NERC Afar and RiftVolc Consortia. Funds for image reproduction were provided by the RCUK Catalyst Seed Fund. I also thank St Anne's College and the University of Oxford for allowing me research leave to complete this project. Some of the themes in this book have developed from posts on my blog, volcanicdegassing; and a part of Chapter 7, on why can't we predict volcanic eruptions, is based on an essay that I originally published in The Conversation.

# BIBLIOGRAPHY

Anderson, A., 'An Account of Morne Garou, a Mountain in the Island of St Vincent, with a Description of the Volcano on its Summit', *Philosophical Transactions of the Royal Society, London*, vol. 75, 1785, pp. 16–31.

Anderson, T. and J.S. Flett, 'Report on the Eruptions of the Soufrière in St Vincent in 1902 and on a Visit to Montagne Pelée', *Philosophical Transactions of the Royal Society, London*, vol. 200, 1903, pp. 353–553.

Anderson, T., *Volcanic studies in many lands*, John Murray, London, 1903.

Anderson, T., *Volcanic studies in many lands,* Second series, ed. T.G. Bonney, John Murray, 1917.

Anon., 'Scientific aspects of the Java catastrophe', *Nature*, vol. 28, 1883, p. 437.

Anon., *A True and Strange Relation of Fire, which by an Eruption brake forth out of the bowels of the earth in the depth of the Sea, and made an Island of foure miles and a halfe in length, one of the Islands of the Tercera's, etc.*, N. Butter and N. Bourne, London, 1639.

Anon., *Wonders! Descriptive of some of the most remarkable of nature and art*, J. Harris and Son, London, 1821.

Blue Book, 'Report from Committee on Petition of Persons interested in estates on Saint Vincent', *Parliamentary Papers by Command*, Cd. 182, HMSO, London, 1813.

Blue Book, 'West Indies. Further correspondence relating to the hurricane on 10th–12th September, 1898, and the relief of distress caused thereby', *Parliamentary Paper by Command* Cd. 9550, HMSO, Darling and Son, London, 1899.

Blue Book, 'Correspondence relating to the volcanic eruptions in St Vincent and Martinique in May 1902, with map and appendix', *Parliamentary Paper by Command*, Cd. 1201, HMSO, Darling and Son, London, 1903.

Blue Book, 'Further correspondence relating to the volcanic eruptions in St Vincent and Martinique in 1902 and 1903', *Parliamentary Paper by Command*, Cd. 1783, HMSO, Darling and Son, London, 1904.

Boswell, J., *Boswell's Life of Johnson*, ed. George Hill, 2nd edn, Clarendon Press, Oxford, 1964–1971, Vol. IV. The Life (1780–1784).

Bristowe, W.S., *A Book of Islands*, G. Bell and Sons, London, 1969.

Bromley, W., *Remarks in the grand tour of France and Italy, performed by a person of quality, in the year 1691*, John Nutt, London, 1705.

Buondelmonti, C., *Liber insularum archipelagi*, Oxford, Bodleian Library, MS. Canon. Misc. 280, c. 1420.

Bylandt-Palstercamp, Comte A de, *Théorie des volcans, Atlas*, 1836. F.G. Levralut, Paris.

Cocco, S., *Watching Vesuvius*, University of Chicago Press, Chicago, IL, 2012.

Dampier, W., *A voyage to New Holland &c. in the year 1699*, James Knapton, London, 1703.

Dampier, W., *Continuation of a voyage to New Holland &c. in the year 1699*, James Knapton, London, 1709.

Darwin, C., *Journal of researches into the natural history and geology of the countries visited during the voyage of HMS Beagle around the world*, John Murray, London, 1845.

Daubeny, C., 'Some account of the eruption of Vesuvius, which occurred in the month of August 1834', *Philosophical Transactions of the Royal Society of London*, vol. 125, 1835, pp. 153–9.

Daubeny, C., *A description of active and extinct volcanos, with remarks on their origin, their chemical phenomena and the character of their products*, W. Phillips, London, 1826.

Defoe, D., *Romances and Narratives*, ed. George Aitken, vol. 15/16, 1895/6.

Dunn, W., *Diary of William Dunn, schoolmaster of Belbroughton, Worcs., 1767–95, including daily reports on the weather*, Oxford, Bodleian Library, MS. Don. c. 76.

Faujas de Saint-Fond, B., *Recherches sur les volcans éteints du Vivarais et du Velay*, Cuchet, Grenoble, 1778.

Fergus, H.A., *Montserrat, History of a Caribbean colony*, Macmillan, Oxford, 2004.

Fergus, H.A., *Volcano Verses*, Peepal Tree Press, Leeds, 2003.

Finch, H., Earl of Winchilsea, *A true and exact relation of the late prodigious earthquake and eruption of Mount Etna or Monte-Gibello*, T. Newcomb, London, 1669.

Foley, S., 'An account of the Giants Caus-Way in the North of Ireland', *Philosophical Transactions of the Royal Society of London,* vol. 18, 1694, pp. 170–82.

Forster, J., *Observations made during a voyage round the world*, Nicholas Thomas, Harriet Guest and Michael Dettelbach (eds), University of Hawaii Press, Honolulu, HI, 1996.

Fritsch, K.W.G. von, J.W. Reiss and A. Stübel, *Santorin, the Kaimeni islands*. Trübner and Co., London, 1867.

Fouqué, F., *Santorin et ses eruptions*, G. Masson, Paris, 1879.

Franklin, B., 'Meteorological imaginations and conjectures', *Memoirs of the Literary and Philosophical Society of Manchester*, December 1784, pp. 373–7.

Geikie, A., 'On modern denudation', *Transactions of the Geological Society of Glasgow*, vol. 3, 1871, pp. 153–90.

Gessner, C., *De rerum fossilium, lapidum et gemmarum*, Tiguri, 1565.

Gilpin, W., *An historical account of the weather during twenty years from 1763–1785*, Oxford, Bodleian Library, MS. Eng. misc. d. 564

Gordon-Cumming, C., *Fire Fountains: the Kingdom of Hawaii, Its Volcanoes and the History of its Missions*, William Blackwood and Sons, Edinburgh and London, 1883.

Goree, Father. 'A relation of a new island which was raised up from the bottom of the sea on the 23rd of May 1707', *Philosophical Transactions of the Royal Society, London*, vol. 27, 1710–1712, p. 356

Graham, M. (ed.), *Voyage of HMS Blonde to the Sandwich Islands in the years 1824–1825*, John Murray, London, 1826.

Hamilton, J., *Volcano*, Reaktion Books, London, 2012.

Hamilton, W., 'A letter from Sir William Hamilton K.B. F.R.S. to Sir John Pringle, Bart. P.R.S. giving an account of certain traces of volcanos on the Banks of the Rhine', *Philosophical Transactions of the Royal Society, London*, vol. 68, 1778, pp. 1–6.

Hamilton, W., 'Two letters from the Hon, William Hamilton, His Majesty's Envoy Extraordinary at Naples, to the Earl of Morton, President of the Royal Society containing an account of the last eruption of Mount Vesuvius', *Philosophical Transactions of the Royal Society, London*, vol. 57, 1767, pp. 192–200.

Hamilton, W., *Campi Phlegraei: Observations on the volcanoes of the two Sicilies*, Naples, 1776.

Hamilton, W., *Supplement to the Campi Phlegraei being an account of the great eruption of Mount Vesuvius in the month of August 1779*, Naples, 1779.

Hawkesworth, J., *An account of the voyages undertaken by the order of His present Majesty for making discoveries in the Southern Hemisphere*, Strahan and Cadell, London, 1773.

Herbert, S., *Charles Darwin: Geologist*, Cornell University Press, Ithaca, NY, 2005.

Hicks, A. and R. Few, 'Trajectories of Social Vulnerability during the Soufrière Hills Volcanic Crisis', *Journal of Applied Volcanology*, vol. 4, 2015, p. 10.

Holmes, A., 'The association of lead with uranium in rock-minerals, and its application to the measurement of geological time', *Proceedings of the Royal Society of London A*, vol. 85, 1911, pp. 248–56.

Humboldt, A. von, *Essai sur la geographie des plantes*, Levrault, Paris, 1805.

Humboldt, A. von, *Vues des Cordillères et monumens des peoples indigènes de l'Amerique*, J. Smith, Paris, 1816.

Humboldt, A. von, *Personal narratives of travels to the equinoctial regions of the new continent, during the years 1799–1804*, Longman, Hurst, Rees, Orme and Brown, London, 1814–1829.

Johnson, R.W., *Fire Mountains of the Islands*, ANU E-Press, Canberra, 2013.

Jorio, A. de, *Ricerche sul Tempio di Serapide in Pozzuoli*, Naples, 1820.

Juan, J. and A. de Ulloa, *Relacion historica del viaje a la America meridional*, Antonio Marin, Madrid, 1748.

Judd, J.W., *Volcanoes: what they are and what they teach*, Kegan, Paul, Trench and Co., London, 1881.

Kaempfer, E., *The history of Japan*, Woodward and Davis, London, 1727.

Keane, Hugh Perry, *Diary*, Virginia Historical Society Mss1 K197 a 23.

Kircher, A., *The Vulcano's or mountains vomiting fire, famous in the World; with their remarkables*, J. Derby, London, 1669.

Kircher, A., *Mundus Subterraneus*, Jansson and Weyerstraten, Amsterdam, 1664.

Knowles Middleton, W. E., 'The 1669 eruption of Mount Etna: Francesco d'Arezzo on the vitreous nature of lava', *Archives of Natural History*, vol. 11, 1982, pp. 99–102.

Krafft, M. *Volcanoes, Fire from the Earth*, Thames and Hudson, London, 1993.

ku'ualoha ho'omanawanui, *Voice of Fire: Reweaving the Literary Lei of Pele and Hi'iaka*, University of Minnesota Press, Minneapolis, MN, 2014.

Lacroix, A., *Montagne Pelée et ses éruptions*, Masson et cie., Paris, 1904.

Ledyard, J., *A journal of Captain Cook's last voyage to the Pacific Ocean, and in quest of a north-west passage etc.*, Nathaniel Patten, Hartford, CT, 1783.

Letter from J.S. Henslow to C. Darwin, 24 August 1831. Darwin Correspondence Project.

Anderson, T., Letters from Tempest Anderson to James Bryce. Oxford, Bodleian Library, MS. Bryce 22.

Logan Lobley, J., *Mount Vesuvius: A descriptive, historical and geological account of the volcano and its surroundings*, Roger and Drowley, London, 1889, pp. 362–5.

Mackenzie, G.S., *Travels in the island of Iceland*, Archibald Constable and Co., Edinburgh, 1812.

Masculus, I.B., *de incendio Vesuvii*, Roncalioli, Naples, 1633.

Molyneux, T., 1698, 'A letter … containing some additional observations on the Giants Causeway in Ireland', *Philosophical Transactions of the Royal Society, London*, vol. 20, 1698, pp. 209–23.

Morris, C., *The Volcano's Deadly Work*, W.E. Scull, Washington DC, 1902.

Müller, J., *Beschreibung der Insel Java*, E. Gross, Berlin, 1860.

Munster, S., *Cosmographiae universalis*, Henricus Petrus, Basel, 1550.

*Navigatio Sancti Brendani*. Oxford, Bodleian Library MS. Laud Misc. 173.

Nomikou, P., M.M. Parks, D. Papanikolaou, D.M. Pyle, T. A. Mather, S. Carey, A.B. Watts, M. Paulatto, L.M. Kalnins, I. Livanos, K. Bejelou, E. Simou and I. Perros 'The Emergence and Growth of a Submarine Volcano: the Kameni Islands, Santorini, Greece', *GeoResJ*, vol. 1–2, 2014, pp. 8–18.

O'Donoghue, D., *Brendaniana: St Brendan the Voyager in story and legend*, Browne and Nolan, Dublin, 1895.

Olaus, M., *Historiae de gentibus septentrionalibus*, G. M. de Viottis, Rome, 1555.

Ortelius, A., *The theatre of the whole world*, Eliot's Court Press, London, 1606.

Ovid, *Metamorphoses, Book XV 335–379*, Translated by A.D. Melville, Oxford University Press, Oxford, 1998.

Parks, M.M., J. Biggs, P. England, T.A. Mather, P. Nomikou, K. Palamartchouk, X. Papanikolaou, D. Paradissis, B. Parsons, D.M. Pyle, C. Raptakis and V. Zacharis 'Evolution of Santorini Volcano Dominated by Episodic and Rapid Fluxes of Melt from Depth', *Nature Geoscience*, vol. 5, 2012, pp. 749–54.

Perret, F.A., *Vesuvio*, Naples, 1906.

Perret, F.A., *The Vesuvius Eruption of 1906: Study of a Volcanic Cycle*, Carnegie Institute of Washington, Washington DC, 1924.

Pliny the Younger, *Letters, Volume I: Books 1–7*, Translated by Betty Radice. Harvard University Press, Cambridge, MA, 1969.

Pyle, D.M. and J.R. Elliott, 'Quantitative Morphology, Recent Evolution and Future Activity of the Kameni Islands Volcano, Santorini, Greece', *Geosphere*, vol. 2, 2006, pp. 253–68.

Raffles, S., *Memoir of the Life and Public Services of Sir Thomas Stamford Raffles*, John Murray, London, 1830.

Raspe, R.E., 'A letter from Mr R.E. Raspe F.R.S. to M. Maty, M.D., Sec.R.S. containing a short account of some Basalt Hills in Hassia', *Philosophical Transactions of the Royal Society, London*, vol. 61, 1771, p. 581.

Richard de Saint-Non, J.C., *Voyage Pittoresque; ou, description des royaumes de Naples et de Sicile*, Clousier, Paris, 1781.

Rudwick, M. J. S., 'Poulett Scrope on the Volcanoes of Auvergne: Lyellian Time and Political Economy', *British Journal for the History of Science* vol. 7, 1974, pp. 205–42.

Rudwick, M.J.S., 'The Emergence of a Visual Language for Geological Science 1760–1840', *History of Science* vol. 14, 1976, pp. 149–95.

Rudwick, M.J.S., *Worlds before Adam*, University of Chicago Press, Chicago, 2008.

Russell, B., *History of Western Philosophy*, Routledge, London, 2004.

St John, J.A., *The history of the Manners of the Ancient Greeks*, Richard Bentley, London, 1844.

Scrope, G.P., *Considerations on Volcanoes*, W. Phillips, London, 1825.

Scrope, G.P., *Memoir on the Geology of Central France*, Longman, Rees, Orme, Brown and Green, London, 1827.

Scrope, G.P., *Volcanos*, Longmans, Green and Reader, London, 1872.

Siebert, L., T. Simkin and P. Kimberley, *Volcanoes of the World*, University of California Press, Berkeley, CA, 2010.

Sigurdsson, H., *Melting the Earth*, Oxford University Press, Oxford, 1999.

Smith, S.D., 'Volcanic Hazard in a Slave Society: the 1812 Eruption of Mount Soufrière in St Vincent', *Journal of Historical Geography*, vol. 37, 2011, pp. 55–67.

Spallanzani, L., *Viaggi alle Due Sicilie e in alcune parti dell' Appennino*, Comini, Pavia, 1792–97.

Stewart, C.S., *Journal of a Residence in the Sandwich islands during the Years 1823, 1824 and 1825*, H. Fisher, Son, and P. Jackson, London, 1828.

Stommel, H. and E. Stommel, *Volcano Weather*, Seven Seas Press, Newport, RI, 1983.

Symons, G.J., 'The Krakatoa Eruption', *Nature*, vol. 29, 1884, p. 355.

Symons, G.J., *The Eruption of Krakatoa and Subsequent Phenomena*, Trübner, London, 1888.

Thorarinsson, S., *Surtsey: the New Island in the North Atlantic*, Viking Press, New York, NY, 1967.

Tillard, S., 'A Narrative of the Eruption of a Volcano in the Sea off the Island of St Michael', *Philosophical Transactions of the Royal Society, London*, vol. 102, 1812, pp. 153–4.

Troil, U. von, *Letters on Iceland &c*, G. Perrin, Dublin, 1780.

Vine, F.J., and D.H. Matthews, 'Magnetic anomalies over oceanic ridges', *Nature*, vol. 199, 1963, pp. 947–9.

Waldie, J., *Sketches Descriptive of Italy in the Years 1816 and 1817, with a Brief Account of Travels in Various Parts of France and Switzerland in the Same Years*, John Murray, London, 1820.

West, S., 'From Volcano to Green Mountain: a Note on Cyrene's Beginnings', *Palamedes*, vol. 7, 2012, pp. 43–66.

White, S., *Diary of The Rev. Sampson White of Maidford, Northants – 1795–1823*, Oxford, Bodleian Library, MS. Eng. misc. d. 241, c. 198.

Witze, A. and J. Kanipe, *Island on Fire: the Extraordinary Story of Laki*, Profile Books, London, 2014.

Wulf, A., *The Invention of Nature*, John Murray, London, 2015.

Young, D.A., *Mind over Magma*, Princeton University Press, Princeton, NJ, 2003.

# INDEX

The explosive eruption of Vesuvius in August 1779, showing a billowing volcanic plume and lightning, and ash and ejecta falling to the ground. © Ashmolean Museum, University of Oxford.

FVRENTIS ANNO MDCCLXXIX VESVVII PROSPECTVS.
FERDINANDO IV. SICILIARVM REG

P. ANTONIVS PIAGGIVS EX SCHOLARVM IARVM CLERICIS REGVLARIBVS.